Entrepreneur's Notebook

Entrepreneur's Notebook

Practical Advice for Starting a New Business Venture

Steven K. Gold

Learning Ventures Press

Entrepreneur's Notebook:
Practical Advice for Starting a New Business Venture

Published by Learning Ventures Press

ISBN-13: 978-1480080041

ISBN-10: 1480080047

Printed in the United States of America

The publisher and author are not engaged in rendering legal, accounting, or other professional services. If you require such services, please consult an appropriately qualified professional.

Dedicated to Deb, Henry and Jenny –

you constantly amaze me

Entrepreneur's Notebook

Contents

Introduction

Entrepreneur's Notebook: Practical Advice for Starting a New Business Venture is written for entrepreneurs and anyone who dreams of becoming an entrepreneur – and who wants real-life advice and practical information. This book will take you on a whirlwind tour of the start-up process and help you to build a solid foundation for your new venture, whether it is a small business, or a venture capital funded enterprise. Irrespective of the size or type of business, the underlying principles are the same.

As an entrepreneur for most of my life, it's impossible to imagine a career more challenging or gratifying. Being an entrepreneur is one of life's great adventures. It allows you to take control of your destiny, continuously learn and grow, and experience the sense of accomplishment that comes with transforming an idea into something of value. Whether you seek to build a large corporation, or create a modest business that will enable you to live the life you choose, this book will guide you through the key steps in the start-up process, helping you to make smart decisions and avoid costly mistakes.

Becoming an entrepreneur is achievable for everyone, but there are rules to the game – principles that are time-tested and likely to lead you to success. This book focuses on the information that you need to know to get started. Chapters 1-3 introduce three critical concepts that relate to every new venture: people, products, and making progress. Chapters 4-5 discuss the entrepreneurial team. In chapters 6-7, a review of the business plan is followed by a discussion of cash flow, a concept that is appreciated by every successful entrepreneur. Finally, chapters 8-10 delve into the practicalities of starting a new company, securing investment, and managing a team of people.

I should note two things about this book. First, it is about concepts, and is not a technical manual. There are many great resources that teach accounting, finance, marketing, management, and more. The real spotlight is on the Big Picture. Second, it focuses on getting your new business off the ground. While the ideas presented are valid and remain important throughout the life of a business, new challenges arise as a business becomes successful, grows, and eventually matures. The later stages rely on a solid foundation and success in the early stages; however a

Introduction

discussion about the development and management of a mature business is beyond the scope of this book.

Starting a company is, without question, both a personal and professional quest. This book is intended to help you to succeed by providing you with advice that is practical and proven, learned the hard way through almost three decades of real-life experience, and backed by the lessons of one of the best business schools in the country. Another reason why this book (and others) will contribute to your success is because sooner is always better than later. You want this information now, before you take action, and an investment of time and dollars in knowledge is small in comparison to the benefits you will receive by making smarter decisions and avoiding the common mistakes. I hope that the following pages inform and inspire you, and help you to realize your entrepreneurial dreams.

Steven K. Gold
Lexington, Massachusetts

Chapter 1
A Wonderful Madness

Just before I started my first significant entrepreneurial venture – one of several that would follow – I became convinced that I was going mad. In retrospect, I probably was mad. I was in my early thirties, uncertain about the future, and doing my best to find some meaning for my professional life. Armed with two degrees (in business and medicine) and a few years of real-life experience in the workforce, I needed to make a drastic change. It was time to prove to myself that I could make a living as an entrepreneur, starting and running my own companies – something that I had always dreamed about. Little did I know that this would be the humble start of a lifelong adventure as a professional entrepreneur.

The reality is that most people are equally well prepared to be successful entrepreneurs. Although I had started a few small ventures in my childhood and also as a young adult, I was still relatively inexperienced at the time that I started my first serious venture – one involving partners and investors. If you already work in a business, have technical expertise, spend time with customers, or have management, sales or marketing experience, for example, then you are miles ahead of where I was when I started. The more experience, knowledge and determination you have, the better prepared you are to succeed.

One's interests often provide a starting point for where one goes in life, especially for an entrepreneur. Two of my interests are biology and business. Although these interests seem worlds apart, they share common features. On a most basic level, biology and business both involve the piecing together of resources to create something new, whether this means molecules combining to create cells and living organisms, or people, ideas and dollars being combined to create a new business. Also, biology and business both have the potential to benefit society. While a new drug or medical technology can help many people, a successful business is certain to have an equally powerful positive impact on the lives of its founders, employees, customers, suppliers, and investors.

My education and interests were the driving forces that led me to start a biotechnology company – the first in a long line of ventures. This business would be a way for me to do some good while pursuing my goals of working for myself and personal financial security. The result was a company that I started with two university researchers who had some unique ideas about how to treat cancer. If they were the brains, I was the brawn, working diligently to transform an idea into a product that would help treat people with cancer – a disease that had taken its toll on my own family. The experience was full of surprises, emotional highs and lows, and also the source of a huge amount of practical information about how to start and grow a new venture. This business, and the many others that I have started and managed since, have provided me with a trial-by-fire education in entrepreneurship, and taken me on a path that ultimately led to the information presented in this book.

As with most entrepreneurial ventures, the unexpected became the expected, and the story of our new company unfolded in unimaginable ways. The venture was a reasonable success. The company was sold about a year after it was started, I made a few dollars as a result, and a new cancer therapy is working its way through the drug development process. This was also the start of my career as a serial entrepreneur – someone who lives fully for the challenge and adventure of entrepreneurship, and who has experienced the start-up and growth of a business at least a few times. Like all entrepreneurs, I thrive on the excitement, energy, and incredible creativity that define the experience. It's all part and parcel of a "Wonderful Madness," an essential and also unavoidable trait shared by most entrepreneurs.

I use the term "Wonderful Madness" because no matter what your age or experience, entrepreneurship involves such things as obsession, compulsion, creative surges, and a roller coaster of emotional highs and lows. All of this can make you appear mad, whether or not it's true.

The life of an entrepreneur does not resemble normal behavior by most people's standards. This may explain why many of your friends give you a blank stare when you tell them you're starting a company, or why you get the sense that family members are talking about you behind your back. Go easy on them. Few of us are fated to be entrepreneurs, or even to understand why anyone else would want to subject himself to all of the risks and hard work. It's difficult for many people to appreciate the appeal of entrepreneurship versus the perception of stability and a regular paycheck that comes with a "real job." The best suggestion is to swallow your pride and concentrate on building your new venture. Ultimately, there is nothing more convincing than success.

The foundation for a start-up venture is the entrepreneur – you. Of course, you are likely to be joined by several team members, possibly including partners, employees and advisors, throughout the course of your adventure. Each of these people will come with their own distinct personality. Throughout my career I have observed many entrepreneurs and have come to recognize three types of entrepreneurial personalities at work. Since people are the most critical part of any new venture, understanding entrepreneurial personalities will not only help you to work with others and build a well-oiled team of people, it will also maximize your chances of success.

The Three Entrepreneurial Personalities

Most entrepreneurs are passionate and driven by a true sense of purpose. For example, some people will become doctors after witnessing, at an impressionable age, their goldfish being flushed down the toilet and regretting not being able to save it (which wasn't the case for me, but in general it happens). It's similar for many entrepreneurs. It's about the goldfish – the loss, pain, or even shame – or whatever it is that motivates a person to pursue success through one's own efforts while assuming more risk and hardship than are experienced working for someone else.

Entrepreneurship involves a particular mixture of drive, pride and self-confidence – a combination that isn't often found in the typical work environment.

For some, the entrepreneurial life provides the possibility to pursue a dream. For others, it provides an alternative to a salaried job that either no longer satisfies, or exists. Some people seek out the experience; others fall into it, not knowing what to expect. No one type of individual makes a better entrepreneur than any other. In fact, all of the personality types play roles in the entrepreneurial process, especially when working together as a team.

I identify three categories of entrepreneurs: Professionals, Pragmatists, and Inventors. Each of these is unique and essential. Some of us fall into one category; most of us are a combination of these three personality types. You will recognize yourself, as well as other entrepreneurs and members of your team, in these descriptions.

1. **Professionals:** These are the individuals who make entrepreneurship their life, whether they start their careers this way, or become entrepreneurs after years in a traditional job. While many Professionals are serial entrepreneurs, starting and growing several ventures over the course of a lifetime, others dedicate

themselves to the long-term success of one company, possibly even transcending some invisible barrier to become respected corporate executives and captains of industry. For the Professional, a strong desire to learn, grow and have fun parallels the need to make each venture a success. While a common image of the Professional entrepreneur is that of a person rising from poverty or other positions of weakness to great heights, more and more the Professional entrepreneur is someone with years of experience, education or training who comes to the realization that the entrepreneurial life offers a few things that virtually no other job ever could: the ability to pursue a special interest, control of one's own destiny, and the possibility of personal financial freedom.

2. **Pragmatists:** These individuals are typically career-oriented professionals who find themselves somehow drawn into an entrepreneurial venture. They are classically well trained by years of experience in the corporate world. Everyone should have at least one Pragmatist on their team. Pragmatists are among the best marketing people, finance experts, and managers – positions that require lots of patience and discipline. Although most Pragmatists have reservations about the uncertainties of an unfunded new venture, they

are usually willing to help from the sidelines during the initial stages, later serving as an invaluable source of high-quality talent once the venture is established. One possibility is to engage a Pragmatist as a part-time consultant for your new venture, working on deferred pay, and with no firm commitment to join the company at first. This will allow you to access solid advice and possibly include his or her name and profile in your business plan. Pragmatists add value and credibility to a start-up, and will commonly do everything within reason to sooner or later join the venture. Once involved with a successful venture, a Pragmatist often finds that she is forever changed, never again able to return to a "regular" job.

3. **Inventors**: The Inventor is someone who slaves away day and night working to make his or her dream a reality – or who dies trying. Inventors are most often endearingly neurotic, driven by the need for attention to their brilliance and brainchild. Most Inventors are single-minded in their goals, borderline geniuses that sometimes turn what they touch into gold. Inventors are guided by conviction, sometimes reality-based but often not. This means that many Inventors face one of two outcomes: going broke or changing the world. Inventor entrepreneurs are responsible for several of

today's leading companies. All of this, however, often comes at a great personal cost, due to their extreme focus and occasional misunderstanding of the "Big Picture" and its practical realities. Many Inventors, for example, start a company only to lose control as enthusiasm gives way to the day-to-day practicalities of operating the business. Other inventors mistake a fortunate discovery for repeatable success – making a fortune and then losing it all in a subsequent failed attempt. When an Inventor does meet with success, he is often portrayed to represent virtues such as hard work, persistence and dedication. The bottom line is that while hard work and creativity both play a role, most successful Inventors share a useful trait with just about every successful entrepreneur: luck.

The majority of start-up ventures will ultimately involve several people as partners, employees, consultants and advisors. Having the right combination of talent, not only in terms of functional expertise such as management, finance, marketing, etc., but also in terms of the three personality types described above, is a critical factor for success. In addition, people who complement and like one another provide a solid foundation for success.

Real-Life Entrepreneurial Profiles

The following profiles describe real people, all of whom I have known over the course of my entrepreneurial life. Their names have been changed, as have some of the details, to respect their privacy. Despite the differences in their stories, their actions and achievements are valuable lessons for all of us.

Professional: Jim is a professional entrepreneur. After he earned a graduate degree in the sciences, he spent a few years working as a consultant – learning a lot about the pharmaceutical industry. After a few years of work with consulting clients, he decided that it was time to start his own company. This is when we crossed paths. I was between ventures, and Jim was just beginning his quest. We soon figured out that we had similar interests, and we frequently discussed our progress and challenges. Jim's first entrepreneurial venture came to a grinding halt when his business partner failed to materialize because she decided to remain employed. A second venture was derailed due to a lucrative consulting engagement. But the third venture took off. Jim learned of a bold idea, one with the potential to create valuable new drugs. The idea remained dormant for a while, and was energized when an investor came onto the scene. This was someone who

Jim had met during a consulting project, and who had profited from Jim's solid advice. The investor liked the entrepreneur's vision, and he put up the seed money. Within a few months, Jim's company was formed and funded. To his credit, he recruited several exceptional partners, mostly experienced Pragmatists. He then began the process of developing and proving the idea. Despite his relative inexperience, Jim knew his strengths and weaknesses, and made the most of his relationships with others. To date, he has raised millions of dollars from a few of the leading venture capital investors. He manages a strong team of competent executives who complement his own skills and abilities. Jim's idea is now being put to the test, and the venture itself is successful and meeting its objectives. Although it will most likely be a few years before any of the company's products reach the market, he has established himself as a skilled entrepreneur, a Professional, as a result of his insight, persistence, choice of co-founders, capable management style, and business accomplishments to date.

Pragmatist: If you've ever dreamed of a co-founder who would be dedicated to all of the details, and there are many details in any new business, then partner with a Pragmatist. These are individuals with the experience and work ethic to get things done, often having spent years learning in the corporate world. A mutual friend introduced me to Anne after she was "downsized" from a large corporation and searching for a new opportunity. She is a financial wizard by training, who also happens to have dabbled in accounting, taxes, human resources, strategic planning and project management. She earned her M.B.A. from a respected business program and is a C.P.A. too. What really impressed me, however, was her energy. Anne not only did lots of things for our new venture, but she seemingly did them all at once. I have never witnessed anything quite like it, and I learned that there is a terrific benefit to having a Pragmatist as your business partner. Although nobody will ever duplicate Anne in my mind, the reality is that most Pragmatists have similar capabilities. Not every Pragmatist can accomplish as much in a four-day work week while caring for two energetic kids and doing her elderly neighbors' taxes for free, but the majority are hard working, experienced, and knowledgeable. To be sure, a Pragmatist does not always feel comfortable with the uncertainties of a start-up venture, but they find ways to work through the challenges. Their corporate upbringing blends a strong work ethic with a dose of diplomacy and professionalism. Give a Pragmatist a mission or objective, and if the job can be done, it will get done. A Pragmatist should be part of every entrepreneurial team.

Inventor: The Professor has two doctoral degrees, and although I refer to him as the "Professor," he has never worked in academia. A mutual friend introduced the two of us, proclaimed the Professor a genius, and indicated that he had some ideas for starting a company. I soon learned that he was indeed intelligent, but that his first concept suffered from a problem associated with many well-intentioned inventions – somebody else had already invented and patented it. In any case, we kept in touch and he contacted me several months later wanting to discuss another idea. This time things looked brighter. Rather than focus on an innovation with which he had little experience, as was originally the case (one reason he missed knowing about the competitor), he described a technology with which he had a 20-year history of practical experience. In fact, he was arguably one of the first people to ever design, build and also operate the particular technology for large-scale applications. After several more meetings, I agreed to help the Professor start a new venture. The Professor is a classic Inventor personality. His enthusiasm for his technology carries him away to the point that he too often forgets the "Big Picture." This often leads to a lack of clear priorities for the business as a whole, and prevents him from being a leader of a company. The great business thinker Peter Drucker has said that one should "never confuse activity with progress." The Professor is always active, but has difficulty making progress for the benefit of the business (rather than for the benefit of one of his scientific ideas – science projects that represent only a small part of the business as a whole). I spent many hours working with the Professor trying to help him to understand the often enormous divide between activity and progress. In due course, the Professor found a Professional entrepreneur to be the CEO of his fledgling company. This has helped him to overcome some of his leadership issues, and the Professor can now focus on what he loves and does best.

While the above stories summarize a few fairly pure entrepreneurial personalities, most of us fit into two personality types. Here are two examples of successful multiple-personality entrepreneurs:

Inventor and Professional: Ella is a superoverachieving technical type. She avidly pursued one graduate degree, left college just before graduation, and then went on to earn another degree in a completely different field. Her work pattern has been the same. First, she worked in one business, then left abruptly and started in another. Her primary skill is self-transformation. She will tell you that she gets bored with things; but she is actually a creative genius who needs to be working on something new all the time. When a concept becomes developed, it's time for Ella to move on. Five years ago, Ella decided to go back to college so she could take some business courses. She immediately recognized the potential to channel her creative energies into new business ventures rather than new careers – in other words, she would become a serial entrepreneur. In the process, her "Professional" attributes became obvious, something that was not apparent when she worked for others. Ella has started three businesses to date. One of these failed after several years of effort. The other two, however, are thriving. She is actively involved as a senior manager of one of these, a company that uses computer technology to help doctors to better care for their patients. This company has a Professional CEO and other senior managers, and Ella serves in two roles that are well-suited for her Inventor-Professional personality type – using her creativity to develop new products for the company, and developing corporate strategy. As for her other business, she is the founder of a small company that markets a simple medical device that she invented. This company also has a Professional CEO. While Ella is primarily an Inventor, by teaming up with others to start companies she has transformed herself into a successful Inventor-Professional who has found a way to make the most of her creative potential.

Pragmatist and Professional: I'll end with James, one of the few truly magical business partners that I've worked with directly. We first met at his wedding in Oxford, England. He and my wife have been friends since their college years. My wife had told me, before I had ever met him, that we would make a great team. Although James and I exchanged only a few words during the festivities, I sensed that I had met a force. James would never think of himself this way, as he's one of the most grounded people that I've ever met, but it's true. Some people have a way with other people, balancing just the right amount of ambition and humility, and he is one of them. James and his wife visited Boston a few months after their wedding, and I volunteered to be their tour guide for a day. After walking around the city in the rain, we settled in for a drink and got to talking. Within just a few hours, a business idea began to emerge. It was an idea that lay at the intersection of our interests: software and science. The idea was to apply some knowledge about biology and genetics to create modular software – programs that could be instantly rearranged to create new applications, like DNA for software developers. Over the next several months, we communicated by email, and spoke on the phone at least once a week. Gradually, things started to fall into place. Rough ideas became clearly defined, and emails were replaced by drafts of a business plan. Our venture was born. Over the course of the several months that followed, the transatlantic flights started, and the intensity began to build. We searched tirelessly for talent, investors, office space, computers, equipment, and everything that separates fantasy from reality. James continued to live an ocean away, was rarely physically present, but was always working and making progress. Once the investment was secured, James and his wife made their move, and he physically joined the venture. By this time, and through his large network, we had already recruited a team and built a prototype. While I was focused on matters like leases, financial projections, and investment, James was all about the people. Our partnership worked because we complemented one another. While James' past skills and experience related to management and marketing of software and web services, my past skills and experience were directed to strategy, planning, finance and investment. He kept our team happy while I was doing the same with our attorneys, investors and partners. The thing that really impressed me, however, was his transformation from a Pragmatist to a Pragmatist-Professional. With years of management experience, James had a way with people. Everyone enjoyed working with him. He could be your partner or boss, as well as a friend, and he would never sacrifice performance in either role. James also revealed the attributes of a Professional entrepreneur, including dedication to the start-up process and comfort with the chaos and uncertainty that surrounds any new venture. The combination proved to be very effective, and James is one of the best entrepreneurial role models I've been fortunate enough to work with.

<u>Your Entrepreneurial Personality</u>

How do you classify yourself? Are you a Professional, Pragmatist or Inventor, or some combination of these? Your answer to this question provides important insights about your strengths and weaknesses, as well as whom you should be seeking out as your business partners. For example, I classify myself as an Inventor-Pragmatist with some learned Professional tendencies. On the one hand, my passion is creativity, whether this means inventing a strategy, product, or company. On the other hand, I've learned that creativity always needs to be balanced with a realistic view of the world. As a result, I enjoy focusing on creative initiatives while collaborating with dedicated Professionals and other Pragmatists to round out a team.

Start-up entrepreneurs require all kinds of people in their lives: Professionals, Pragmatists, and Inventors. Every start-up venture benefits from a Professional, and many Inventors dream of the day that they can hand over their creation to a Professional entrepreneur. Pragmatists keep people and things straight and provide a necessary day-to-day reality check. If something goes off course, they often know it first and can usually figure out how to fix it. And Inventors, although challenging to work with and often needing reminders about business versus creative realities, sometimes have ideas that really can change the world. The bottom line is that all of the personality types discussed – Professionals, Pragmatists, and Inventors – are important. Most start-up companies will benefit from the contributions of all three of these personality types.

Chapter 2
The Big Idea

My father once told me that the worst mistake anyone can make in business is to be in the wrong business. It took me too many years to comprehend the meaning of his words. Like many entrepreneurs, I initially believed that ideas alone provided a foundation for any great business enterprise – come up with a great idea and the investors, customers and rewards would follow. How about Henry Ford, Thomas Edison, Alexander Graham Bell, or the Wright Brothers, all glorified for their ideas and the industries that they launched? I enthusiastically pursued various inventions and schemes, secured a few patents, and spent a lot of time trying to convince others of their value, ultimately without a lot of success.

The unfortunate problem with this approach is that we, as entrepreneurs committed to an idea, often overlook a key principle: we are not the customer. We are rarely in a position to objectively assess the value of a product or service that we've dreamed up until we settle down and listen to living, breathing customers. So how does the process usually go? Fearful of being stung by reality, we tell our best friend about our new idea. Instantly and without question, he or she loves it, and offers to buy whatever we're selling. We are on the top of the world, and perhaps only moments away from committing our life savings to the shredder.

Now let's back up and review this scenario in slow motion. First, it's unlikely that a best friend (or a spouse or relative) is capable of giving us objective feedback, let alone an honest opinion – especially considering the way we reacted the last time they shared their honest feelings about one of our bright ideas. Furthermore, our personal cheerleader is not likely to be a real customer, or even likely to resemble the average buyer of the proposed product or service. Finally, it's very doubtful that we described our new product or service in a complete and honest manner, fully disclosing both its advantages and disadvantages (assuming these are even known).

If you tell people that you've come up with a new fuel additive that will triple any car's mileage, they will tell you that they'll buy a garage-full. If you disclose the full picture, however, their reaction might be different. For example, this new fuel additive costs half the price of a tank of gas, its use requires a slight modification to one's engine, and it's only about five years and an estimated $4 billion away from reality. In theory, it might work.

As soon as we introduce real ideas to real customers, things change – a lot. All of a sudden, the virtual backlog of hypothetical orders dwindles to a realistic figure, and the entrepreneur is left alone to ponder the future. Fortunately, the future is often bright, but it requires common sense, a lot of hard work, and a healthy dose of pragmatism and good luck to get there.

Returning to the wisdom introduced in the beginning of this chapter, it is essential to pursue a business that is the "right" business. So, how can an entrepreneur determine if a business is the right one? There are several ways to go about the decision. In all cases, the process involves common sense, and a few other concepts that you can use to shift the game to your advantage.

Finding the Right Business

Common sense is a challenge for most of us, so let's start with this. First, don't do anything stupid. This includes any scheme that is impossible or otherwise contrary to the laws of nature. For example, a venture that seeks to design and build spaceships is probably not within the realm of most budding entrepreneurs. Any undertaking involving billions of dollars, or much smaller amounts (all things being relative), may be unreasonable. Cross these ideas off your list. Even a simple widget may take a lot of investment and expertise to get from the drawing board to retail stores, so respect your limitations. If you can't see realistic solutions to the obvious problems, let alone the cadre of lesser challenges, then the idea is probably not meant to be.

Next, stay within the law. One of my all-time favorite business scams was a highly publicized and frequented precious metals store that sold investment grade gold or silver coins at highly competitive prices, and then offered to keep the purchase in their vault for a small monthly fee. Many wealthy and otherwise intelligent people fell for this service, which was in business for years. Its downfall came when someone (I think it was the attorney general) discovered that the owners were reselling the same gold and silver kept in their vault – again and again! This is an example of a profitable business model, but one that is illegal. Go straight to jail! Do yourself a favor and don't do anything stupid or illegal.

Third, be practical. This is just another way of saying that just because you can do something doesn't mean that you should be doing it. Many entrepreneurs have invested awesome amounts of time and money to design, build and sell an extraordinary product, only to learn, about a year later that they've run out of cash. Being practical means that you understand and appreciate the resources that are required to succeed – and have access to them. One of the biggest disappointments for an entrepreneur is arriving at the brink of success – a big sale or grand opening – at the same time that it becomes clear that the business won't work. Find out how much even a simple venture will cost in dollars and time commitment *before* you dive into it. A cash flow analysis is the best way to determine how much cash you will actually need (this basic concept is introduced in Chapter 7).

A real-life example of this was my involvement in the start-up of a small candy company. Simple idea: candy in a package. Most people who were aware of the company during its inception couldn't take it all too seriously – one person said that it resembled a high school fundraising project. After all, how hard could it be to manufacture and sell hard candy? The reality is that a great deal of planning and investment were required to create a company that could grow quickly and become a scalable success. For example, substantial investment was made in creating and refining the product itself, and testing it with real customers all along the way. Several hundred pounds of candy were made for market testing – prior to selling to a single customer. The packaging, a composite can with label, required endless hours of design, market testing and refinement, not to mention four vendors. All of this required substantial resources. Anyone can put candy in a package, but few companies know how to put millions of pieces of candy into thousands of packages a year while making a profit. Even a concept that appears simple can turn out to be quite complex. Get a sense of the practical realities of your proposed venture before committing resources to it.

Finally, listen to intuition. By this, I really mean listen to your spouse, your family, and your friends – not their compliments, but their seemingly off-the-cuff criticism. Keep your ego locked away, and don't interrupt. At the very least, these people are giving you their honest opinion, and are likely to communicate the same issues or objections that will immediately come to the minds of future customers or investors. Take it like an adult, and use the information to learn and grow. It may not be expert advice, but it represents real feedback from people you respect, and it could save your hide.

One of the first reactions an entrepreneur often gets is, "could you please repeat that" or "I'm not quite sure I understand." This should raise some red flags. Do not attempt to explain it further, or convince the other person that he or she is a moron, especially if that person is your spouse. The correct response is to go back to the drawing board. If you can't explain what you intend to do in plain English (or any other language for that matter), then problems lie ahead. Along similar lines, if you can't figure out what your business is, and you can't describe it in one or two sentences, then it's time to keep working on it.

Consider the following business descriptions:

A) Interior Architectural Enhancements Corporation is the developer of sales and marketing outlets that extend interior architectural value through a range of products and services. We leverage more than 100 years of industry experience to provide clients with fully integrated and optimized design consultation and product support, including representation of all leading vendors in the industry. Our selection and knowledge are the best in the business.

B) Wallflower is a chain of shopper-friendly retail stores specializing in quality paints and wall coverings.

They could both be descriptions of the same business. Which of these companies would you frequent, support, or want to invest in? If you can't describe your business idea clearly and concisely – in a sentence or two – then go back to the beginning. You need to know what your new company will do, and it is critical that you are able to effectively communicate this information to others.

Now that we understand a few of the criteria that will hopefully help us to rule out problematic business ideas, let's consider how to find good business opportunities – the ones that should be more seriously explored.

Personal Experience: Despite obvious issues associated with anyone's opinion about their own bright ideas (a lack of objectivity comes to mind), especially when that person happens to be an entrepreneur in overdrive, personal experience is an excellent source of business ideas for two reasons. First, our experiences highlight life's many practical problems, at work and at play, and these problems could be beacons of opportunity. Second, because we generally pursue activities that interest us, especially outside of work, our personal experiences can lead to business product or service ideas that also interest us, and ignite our enthusiasm. Although this may at first seem like a superficial consideration, it isn't. Enthusiasm, motivation, and determination are all key components of entrepreneurial success. Without them, a new venture will fail. The majority of entrepreneurial businesses arise from personal experience. That being said, these ideas require testing, more testing, possible revision, and clear validation from prospective customers.

Key Resource Availability: Another consideration that will help you to evaluate if a business opportunity is a good one for you involves the availability of all critical resources. By this, I mean that if you can't reliably access all of the people, cash, skills, etc. that you will need, then refine or reconsider your idea. On the other hand, if you are fortunate to have access to something of real value that could accelerate your success, then don't ignore it. Evaluate if you have any of the following resources: 1) specific experience, skills or talents, 2) a readily available product or service, or 3) a turnkey business opportunity. The first of these is especially important. If you, or people you intend to have as your partners, have spent endless years in a particular industry and know everything there is to know about the industry, then don't overlook this. Next, the availability of a product or service is another opportunity that should not be ignored – in fact, consider making it the focus of your venture. For example, let's say that you're on vacation in Europe and come across an incredible product – something that is not available in the U.S. You contact the manufacturer and learn that they'd be pleased to work with you – assuming that you would start a company, purchase an inventory of product, and handle all of the details. Of course, similar opportunities may exist closer to home. Finally, a turnkey business could be a great option. This can be a franchise, purchase of an existing business, or spin-off from an established company. A franchise can be a decent option for a person who wants to be self-employed and enjoy the reputation and training offered by a franchisor (note that there are many franchises available and that some are better than others – be sure to investigate any franchise thoroughly before you invest any money into it.) Alternatively, the purchase of an existing business could prove to be a great opportunity for an individual with operating experience who has either the cash to purchase the business, or else the credibility to convince the current owner, a bank, or investors to finance the acquisition. In some cases, a turnkey business can arise when an employee seeks to spin-out a new business from an existing company, or take over ownership of an existing company. Such an opportunity might even be financed by the present employer or owner. In any case, don't ignore readily accessible resources and opportunities.

Market Research/Testing and Validation: Once you have an idea for a business venture, then it's extremely important to test its viability. You need to determine if customers are going to buy your product or service, and if investors will bet their dollars on your unproven company. There are several ways to test the market, some simple and relatively inexpensive, and others only to be attempted by trained professionals. The simple methods are: speaking with lots of people, especially prospective customers (key decision makers, in particular); reading anything and everything that relates to your proposed venture, including industry and market reports, trade journals, public company disclosures, etc.; performing internet searches; and observing your competitors up close and speaking with both them and their customers. To be sure, there are many techniques, several good books on the subject of market research, and quite a few consultants and companies anxious to take your money to conduct focus groups or provide you with data. Most successful entrepreneurs do their own market research. In general, if you don't perform at least some of the market research yourself, then you're unlikely to have the knowledge or credibility to succeed. While it may seem tedious, researching your market is a valuable and often enjoyable experience that should not be overlooked.

Finally, consider what you need to prove to yourself about your business idea? How can you be sure that it will work? Of course, there are no guarantees, but each step, every piece of knowledge and experience, increases the probability of your success, often, in large part, by reducing the probability of failure. Even if you actually do everything right, a little good luck goes a long way. (When interviewing new captains, the shipping magnate Aristotle Onassis would conclude every interview with the question "Are you lucky?") Since you arguably can't control your luck, do what you can to prevent mistakes and tip the scale of success in your favor. Beyond the skills and experience that you bring to the table, reliable information is always extremely helpful.

Practically speaking, there are a few key results that you will seek from your market research. First, you should expect to learn if customers really exist, or if the market is actually a mirage. Second, market research will teach you a lot about the relevant economics. Can you realistically sell something to the customer at a price that will allow you to make an acceptable profit and also to provide a respectable return to your investors? If not, go back to the drawing board. Finally, what is the competition up to? Who are they and how are they really doing? If they are successful, do they have the ability and smarts to squash you like a bug? Are they working on an updated version of their product that will compete more effectively with yours? On the other hand, if they are suffering, is it because they are not meeting customer expectations or because the entire industry is depressed? The bottom line is that you must confirm, with some degree of certainty, that your proposed new venture can 1) deliver the goods, 2) effectively compete for real customers, and 3) make a profit. We will explore each of the three elements of our reality check in more detail – after a few words about generating new business ideas.

Brainstorming for New Business Ideas

Brainstorming takes many forms. While you may be lucky enough to know what business opportunity is best for you, it's much more likely that you're still exploring. A great way to generate interesting ideas is to conduct a brainstorming session – either independently or with a group of people. It's not only fun to do, but surprisingly powerful. The goal of brainstorming (for our purposes) is to create a list of new business ideas for further thought and evaluation. It can be used to generate completely new ideas, or to improve upon an existing one.

The Big Idea

Consider brainstorming with your business partners, or possibly a few creative friends. By the end of the exercise, you will have generated dozens of ideas, all of which will then require some form of market research or validation. Many ideas will be impractical due to the unavailability of required capital, expertise or for other reasons; other ideas will merit further consideration. These represent products and services that may lead to a real opportunity and should be taken to the next step.

Consider the following 5-step brainstorming process:

1. Develop a set of initial criteria by listing specific resources, expertise, limitations, and goals.

2. Pick a starting point. This could be an industry, interest, or a problem that you want to solve. Divide your starting point into its components. Repeat this step. At each step, evaluate your list according to your criteria, eliminating some items and focusing on others.

3. Using your short list, write down as many problems associated with each item as you can think of. Rate the problems and create a new, prioritized list of them. The problems may

represent opportunities. In other words, if you find solutions, customers may be willing to pay for these – thus they may lead you to possible business opportunities.

4. Brainstorm a list of solutions.

5. Based on these solutions to the problems, brainstorm possible business opportunities.

Here's a summary of a brainstorming session performed by a team of food service entrepreneurs:

1. First, the team came up with its criteria:

    •   <u>Expertise</u>: We want to leverage the existing experience of our team in the restaurant/food service business

    •   <u>Resources</u>: We need to be able to launch the business for a reasonable investment; all of us are willing to be full-time employees and to manage the venture

- <u>Limitations</u>: No interest in starting or operating a sit-down or traditional restaurant; Wish to limit our hours in order to spend more time with our families; Products or services need to provide substantial profit margins

- <u>Goals</u>: Build a successful business in 5 years and then sell it to an established operator

2. Then the team decided that the "type" of food service operation was a good starting point. They created the following list. Note that it has several overlapping categories (the team just wrote down their ideas as they came) and is in no particular order.

  - Fast food
  - Take-out
  - Traditional
  - High-end
  - Drive-thru
  - Counter service
  - Cafeteria
  - Full service
  - Specialty food
  - Organic

- Catering
- Soup & Salad bar
- Pizza
- Health food
- Bakery

Next, they reviewed this list and, with their initial criteria in their minds, eliminated some items and focused on others. Here is the revised list with a few comments:

- ~~Fast food~~
- Take-out – possibility if hours are limited – how?
- ~~Traditional~~
- ~~High-end~~
- Drive-thru – keep this in mind
- Counter service – also possible
- Cafeteria – also possible
- ~~Full service~~
- ~~Specialty food~~
- ~~Organic~~
- Catering – not great, but may consider
- Soup & Salad bar – possible focus due to ease?
- Home cooked – nobody's doing this in our area!

- ~~Pizza~~
- ~~Health food~~
- ~~Bakery~~

In general, the group focused on operations that would allow them to a) minimize their initial cash investment, b) differentiate their business from traditional restaurants and popular "fast food" operations, and c) allow them to achieve their objective of more reasonable hours (all of these people had spent years in the business, enjoying most every aspect of it except for the long hours).

3. Next, the group brainstormed a list of the most serious problems associated with some of the categories on their list – focusing on take-out operations. The objective was to list the major problems that came to mind.

   Here is a sampling:

   - Many small, higher quality take-out operations (versus the usual popular fast food chains) are not conveniently located, despite the fact that the primary reason for a take-out purchase is convenience

- Many customers view take-out as more expensive than a home-cooked meal, and regard this higher cost as a trade-off for convenience

- Standing in line and waiting for service deters repeat business, especially in high volume areas, which is compounded by parking or other access difficulties

Here is a summary of the major problems, which have also been prioritized:

1. Convenient access
2. Reasonable price (for the quality level)
3. Efficient service

4. The group then listed their solutions to each of the three major problems that they came up with:

- Convenient access requires a location that customers will naturally pass by, either on foot or in their cars. A few location ideas:
  - City/town center
  - Lobby of large office tower

- o Public transportation hub
- o Drive through location

- Reasonable price means that prices must be favorable relative to the alternatives – other restaurants and take-out operations, as well as home-cooked meals (indirect competition). Here are a few ideas as to how this issue might be addressed:
  - o Menu and service that exceeds customer expectations for the price
  - o Unique offerings that are not typically found at other take-out places, and which are inconvenient to prepare at home
  - o A menu that focuses on one type of food, enabling us to purchase in bulk and pass the savings along to our customers
  - o Creating the perception of great value irrespective of the actual price point
  - o Effective use of coupons and other promotions to provide consumers with discounts and a sense that they are receiving a good value

- Efficient service will be a challenge, since much of the business is likely to occur during two-

hour periods during lunch and the end-of-day
commute. Here are a few possibilities to
address this challenge:
- o Streamlined menu
- o Self-service
- o Fully prepared meals
- o Pick-up only
- o Advance (e.g., online) ordering

5. Finally, the group generated a list of business
   ideas based on this simple analysis. Here are a
   few of them:

- Take-out counter located in the lobby of a large
  office tower that provides a daily menu of three
  fully prepared, home-cooked meals. The simple
  menu enables fresh, quality meals to be sold at
  a relatively low cost, while minimizing waste
  and maximizing profit margins. Meals could be
  prepared at a commercial kitchen off-site to
  keep costs low. Customers can pre-order
  dinners (via a website) for convenient pick-up
  on their way home from the office.

- Small, drive-through location specializing in a
  limited menu of BBQ chicken and ribs, as well

as a selection of pre-packaged (ready-to-serve) side dishes and bottled drinks. Various menu "special deals" for individuals and families streamline pricing and provide customers with a sense of value for the price.

- Pick-up counter located in the city's major commuter station. Customers order their high quality prepared dinners using the internet (or an 800 number), get a pick-up confirmation, and have orders charged to an on-file credit card. Rapid counter pick-up.

All of the possibilities listed above describe interesting business opportunities that meet or exceed the group's initial criteria. In fact, each of these requires minimal build-out costs relative to a full-scale restaurant, and all could be expanded as a chain or franchise in the future. These ideas need to be refined and validated. Depending on the results of the team's market research, and also the amount of investment required, a final decision will be made, or else more ideas will be generated. Nevertheless, these entrepreneurs are off to a good start and are likely to identify an opportunity.

<u>Putting Your Idea to the Test</u>

Once you've come up with a business idea, or a list of ideas, it's necessary to validate them. In essence, you will need to answer three questions to your satisfaction:

1. Can I deliver the goods?
2. Can I compete effectively for customers?
3. Can I make a profit?

Can you deliver the goods? Can you really do what you say that you are going to do? This is the essence of one's ability to deliver the intended product or service. Do you and your team have the expertise to manufacture, market and sell the product or service? Are the results achievable within a reasonable period of time? Do you have access to the human capital, cash and other resources that will be needed to transform your plan into reality? If the answer to any one of these questions is "no," then go back and revise the business plan. Address all anticipated problems before they become real ones. If the answer continues to be "no," then you should seriously consider exploring other business ideas and options. Keep in mind that there is no shame in cutting your losses and moving on, in which case you've made a smart decision and also learned something in the process. On the other hand, if you decide to venture forth knowing that problems exist, then don't be surprised if things don't work out.

Although an affirmative response to the three questions requires detailed thought and planning, there are a few key indicators of possible success, all of which regard the people who are starting the venture. Simply put, it helps a lot if the founders have verifiable credentials relevant to the proposed venture. Although this may involve formal degrees, much more importantly it means that each of the co-founders has the experience, expertise, contacts, solid reputations, and strong desire to succeed. In addition, the team needs to be complete (or provide assurances that this will be so within an appropriate period of time), and cooperation and coordination among the team members should be evident. If you have a team of partners and employees who fit this description, the probabilities are increased that you will be successful.

When it comes to entrepreneurship, exceptions occur frequently. Many successful entrepreneurs do not fit the mold when it comes to the characteristics described above. These people are survivors, determined to succeed despite a lack of experience, education, or reputation (perhaps the result of a past failed business venture). The universal factors for these individuals are the ability to learn from the past, sheer determination to succeed, and a focus on the future – every day providing these people with a new opportunity for accomplishment. Many of these "unqualified" entrepreneurs have disproved the armchair critics and created successful enterprises.

Can you compete effectively for customers? Will customers purchase your product or service versus that of the competition? An ability to compete is paramount to the success of any new venture. While it is often a straightforward matter to learn about customers and what they are looking for (including why they like or dislike the competition), being able to deliver a better product or service is never trivial. In general, knowing and understanding your competition will help you to spot the opportunity, or lack thereof. Some competitors are so smart and strong that it will not make sense to challenge them head-on, should you decide to challenge them at all. Of course, many entrepreneurs find ways to succeed despite powerful competition and a competitor's seemingly endless resources.

There are reasons why virtually every product or service 1) has competition, and 2) should have competition. First, no product or service is 100% essential, and as such, any prospective buyer could simply say, "no – I'm not interested." The "no" generally arises because a customer either plans to purchase somebody else's product or service (direct competition), or a customer would rather spend her money elsewhere or simply hold onto her dollars (two forms of indirect competition). We all make choices about how to spend our money, including the decision not to spend it at all. Your product or service needs to be good enough to overcome these barriers.

Although a poor product or strong competitor can lead to a "no," one interesting reason why customers say "no" is because your product or service may be facing up against intangible factors such as switching cost. For example, let's suppose that you have invented a better mousetrap, but 1) most people have a few inferior mousetraps that are "just fine," and 2) replacing the traps that they own will be a big nuisance (meaning that there is a switching cost). Therefore, your superior mousetrap that sells for a fraction of the cost of an old-style trap is not of much interest to customers. If intangible costs are a barrier to sales, consider ways around them. For example, although most car buyers already own a car in reasonable working condition, the auto industry has managed to find ways to drive demand for new car purchases. Some of these techniques are: design changes that make older models appear obsolete, gradual improvements in features and efficiency, special financing deals, and offers that appear almost too good to be true. Returning to our mousetrap example, it's possible that an imaginatively designed "supertrap" that is marketed the right way could convert a "no" into a "yes." Great marketing goes a long way.

Second, and of greater consequence to us as start-up entrepreneurs, it is often helpful to have competition. Competition indicates the existence of customers and provides you with a benchmark. Customers like to make decisions by comparison. The trick is to determine which characteristics of your product or service you are able to improve upon in the eyes of customers – by learning what customers value. If you're creating a new product or service, it can be challenging to know what features to include or leave out. Competition provides a benchmark from which you can design and test your own product or service (without competitive products or services, you're flying blind). Some obvious improvements may include a lower price, better features, nicer appearance, or more convenience. Less obvious factors may include creative marketing or a simplified purchase process. In fact, many successful ventures have been founded on the basis of better distribution of products (especially commodity products that are otherwise identical to those being sold by the competition), better warranties or return/exchange policies (contributing to the success of several progressive retail chains), and better service. It's amazing what a toll-free phone number along with a pleasant greeting and voice can do, although they do come at a cost. This last point is crucial to appreciate. Most anyone can think of ways to make something better, but at what cost? The goal is to balance costs and benefits in a way that works for customers while also improving your bottom line.

Competitive strategy is the subject of many books. The concept of competitive differentiation, for example, is truly important to most businesses, and learning more about the concept is a worthwhile use of time. Rather than delve into an academic discussion of the topic, which is prone to make a simple concept more complex than it needs to be for purposes of an introduction, here are some examples of competitive strategies:

- Have you ever noticed that some automobile brands look virtually identical to another brand? Automobile companies are true experts at making similar products appear different. Two brands of automobile could employ many of the identical components, yet be marketed under different brand names and at vastly different prices. For example, General Motors make Chevrolet models with relatively few bells and whistles, while its Cadillac automobiles appeal to luxury customers. Yet, both of these brands appear to share similar design elements and components. Of course, the manufacturers of many other products use this same approach. In essence, they segment the market, dividing it into categories of customers. Then, they figure out how to create a product or service that best addresses the needs of each unique market segment. Many smart companies target only one (or a few) market segments. The reason is that it is very difficult to do everything for everyone. By dividing up the market, and determining what smaller groups of customers really want, you can give it to them and succeed in the process. Attempts to please every customer all of the time are prone to failure, especially for a young company with limited resources.

- Some airlines are notorious for poor quality of service. On the other hand, there are a few airlines that stand out, not because they've fixed all of the issues surrounding air travel, but rather because they have found the right balance of features. In other words, these companies have found a way to competitively differentiate their service from the competition. For example, some airlines have developed user-friendly websites to effectively bypass the traditional reservation systems and simplify ticket purchases and seat assignments. In the process, they have lowered their costs and passed some of the savings on to customers. On the other hand, there are some airlines that charge premium prices for a premium level of service. Of course, several airlines manage to charge high prices and provide poor service – a balance that isn't compatible with long term success. The point is that there are different types of customers (unique market segments), and successful airlines cater to one (or a few) market segments with just the right balance of features.

- Businesses that sell commodity-like products can competitively differentiate themselves by creating a unique image or perception about their product or service. Innovative marketing and advertising can convince customers that a product or service is better, faster or cheaper, when it really isn't. For example, while one diamond company suggests that its products last for an infinitely long period of time (diamonds, like everything else, actually degrade over a long period of time), they're really selling the perception of permanence and value. Several premium watch makers sell precision well beyond what the human mind can perceive, yet many consistently late consumers gladly pay for this. Of course, image is important for more than just luxury products. Why do some of us use one overnight delivery service versus another at half the price? Is there a difference between brands of table salt? How much better are premium bottled waters from other, less expensive bottled waters? Consumers would be horrified if they knew that most bottled water is subject to fewer health regulations than tap water. The reality, of course, is that customers who purchase these products do not buy permanence, precision, speed, quality, or taste, but rather the perception of permanence, precision, speed, quality, or taste. This is smart marketing and effective branding (although it can push ethical limits, at times). Although there are differences in many of these products or services, these are often not significant in real terms, but customers will nevertheless pay a large premium for a certain logo or brand. Luxury goods, clothes, footwear, and many other products and services depend on differentiation based predominately on perception. One's ability to use perception to market a product can be very profitable.

- Don't always think that you need to make your product or service "better" than the competition. Many successful entrepreneurs recognize this and intentionally make and sell inferior products by positioning them to appeal to large, often ignored segments of a market, most often at a lower price point. Not every customer wants the best, or can pay the most. For any product or service, there are factors that most every customer expects. For example, coffee needs to be palatable, and paint should adhere to a surface. That being said, there are many people who are proud to be cheap, will happily and repeatedly buy a cup of OK-tasting coffee, or an inexpensive brand of paint that lasts for only half the time of a leading brand (but nevertheless longer than they plan to own their home). Going back to the airline example, a small snack or inedible food is a business decision for these airlines – it's cheaper than a four-star meal and the lower ticket prices fill seats. If you want the four-star meal, then fly first class on a first class airline, or else bring your own. Competitive differentiation simply means that your product or service offers a unique combination of features that are appreciated and valued by one or more segments of the total potential market.

Can you make a profit? Profit is the common language of every successful business. In essence, it means that 1) your customers, whether they are individual consumers or other businesses, place a higher overall value on your products or services than those sold by the competition, and 2) that the total cost to deliver your products or services is lower than your selling price. The "total cost" needs to include the cost to manufacture, market, sell and distribute your product, including overhead, returns, bad debt, and much more. The selling price is *your* selling price – what you actually receive for each unit you sell. Profitability means that you are doing something right, and long-term profitability is the ultimate success.

It should be mentioned that in rare instances profit might not be necessary or even desired. These are specialized situations when an entrepreneur works to position a new venture itself as the product. For example, some "high technology" ventures are established to research and develop a risky new technology. Although a few of these companies will eventually go on to sell products, others will never seek to sell anything (they may say this, but it's not their actual intent). Instead, these companies are started and grown so that they can be sold. For example, such a business might bring together several engineers to design and build a prototype of a product, and then seek to be acquired by a larger company. Another example might be a real estate project. Investors might put money in a company to design and build an office building with the sole intention that the company or its assets will be sold outright. Being acquired by a larger company is a viable business strategy for some (but not most) ventures. Many entrepreneurs with access to venture capital are expert at this risky game of big fish swallows little fish.

When you consider the type of venture you're going to start, you should also think about your exit strategy. This is the term used by investors to describe how they will ultimately get their money back, and how you will possibly earn your payoff. Even if you are not intending to seek any funds from others, you should nevertheless consider yourself as an investor in your own venture. Exit strategy is important for two reasons. First, certain types of ventures are more or less conducive to specific exit strategies. Second, the exit strategy will help you to determine if outside investment is required at all, and if so, will determine the types of investors who will work with you. For example, if you are planning to start a retail venture with a single location where you hope to work for many years, then earning a living in the form of a salary is likely to be your primary exit strategy. In other words, you want to earn a reasonable pay check from the business, maybe take home some extra "profits" every so often, and possibly sell the business or pass it on to a family member in the distant future. If this is the case, your investment will likely come from your own savings, from friends and family, and possibly a local bank. At the opposite end of the financing spectrum is the team of software engineers who seek to raise millions of dollars in venture capital for their high technology start-up. They require lots of employees and equipment to transform a complicated idea into a product quickly, and they need serious financial backing to accomplish this. Their logical financing source will be professional venture capital firms. These firms invest larger sums of money, along with their expertise, to help make a business successful. This team's definition of success, however, differs from that of our retail entrepreneur. Venture capitalists that put money into a venture only do so when they know how they are going to get their money out, and at a significant profit. There are only two serious options for such a venture: being acquired or going public. In practice, this means that the business will be sold to a larger company and/or competitor, or shares (ownership interest) will be sold to the public. In either case, the venture capitalists most often expect to completely exit their investment and receive cash for their shares.

Is one strategy better than another? There are a few ways to answer this question. First, your capabilities should drive the business you seek to enter, which should in turn drive the investment and exit strategies. If you start by thinking that you want to do an IPO, then you are getting ahead of yourself and may be setting yourself up for failure. Second, neither approach is inherently better than the other. The success of either strategy will be much more dependent on the success of the underlying business than whether you seek a paycheck, periodic profit or dividend payments, sale of the entire business, or an IPO. For example, let's say that you start a retail store with minimal resources, build it into a chain of ten stores over five years without incurring much debt, and sell the business for $5 million in the fifth year, before taxes. Your best friend starts a high technology venture with five other colleagues. Her initial 16.67% stake (one-sixth of the initial shares) is diluted by an incentive stock plan (20%), first round venture capital investment (40%), second round of venture capital investment (33%), and an additional 5% dilution when the company is forced to hire a new CEO. This ultimately leaves her with a 5.1% stake in her company. The company goes public with a value of $100 million, making her stake worth about $5.1 million. Although this example is an oversimplification, and involves relatively large numbers, it makes the point that neither strategy is inherently advantageous. Egos aside and generally speaking, you should do what you do best, and the rewards will follow.

The Bottom Line: Making Your Big Idea a Success

The bottom line is that your business idea needs to meet two basic criteria. First, it should be right for you (and your partners). This is often the most challenging part of creating a new business, determining where your skills and abilities best intersect with a particular product or service idea. Second, your product or service needs to be right for a group of prospective customers. This involves design of your product or service in a manner that will set your business apart from the competition while also keeping costs under control – enabling profitability.

During the process of discovering your own Big Idea, use your intuition – but don't lose track of reality. Do what feels right, and what motivates you, but also market test your concepts on real-life customers. Your enthusiasm, the existence of customers for your product or service, and an understanding of the market potential and costs involved, will all contribute to a solid foundation.

At the end of the day, being in the right business means being true to yourself and your customers.

Chapter 3
Stone Soup for the Entrepreneur's Soul

There's been a lot of chicken soup flowing, thanks to the Chicken Soup publications by Jack Canfield and his co-authors. In fact, these books are one of publishing's great entrepreneurial success stories. There is, however, at least one more soup-inspired story to tell. It is a folk tale that goes back many generations. Few stories offer such great insights into the entrepreneurial process.

The Story of Stone Soup

Once upon a time, three soldiers, weary from years of battle in a far off land, were making their way home together through the countryside. As evening arrived and they approached a small village, hunger overcame them. The villagers, wary of all strangers, especially soldiers, were not exactly forthcoming with their food or hospitality. Despite the soldiers' pleas, they were turned away from every door, and villagers peered from their windows to keep a close eye on the three of them.

The soldiers retreated to the town green to ponder their situation. Some time passed. "I have it!" exclaimed the first soldier, who proceeded to tell the others about his recipe for Stone Soup. A few minutes later, the second soldier loudly announced to the villagers within earshot, "Since you have not enough food to share, we are going to make Stone Soup. Come join us, and you are very welcome to have some yourselves!" Several curious villagers left the comfort of their homes and gathered around the three soldiers on the village green.

"To start, we will need a big pot," said the first soldier. A few men went off in search of an oversized iron cauldron – and returned with one a few minutes later. "Next we will need some water," exclaimed the second soldier. Off went several other villagers. "And some wood please," requested the third soldier, who led a small group off into the nearby woods. When all was assembled, with fire blazing and water boiling, the first soldier cleared his throat and spoke, "Finally ladies and gentlemen, we will need three large and perfectly round stones!" Intrigued, the remaining villagers scurried off into the surrounding woods to the local stream, and returned with three large and perfectly round stones. With great fanfare each of the stones was carefully placed into the pot. The Stone Soup was now underway.

After several minutes, the first soldier tasted the Stone Soup. "Delicious!" he said loud enough for all around to hear, "but it would be even better with salt and pepper – and some spices perhaps!" A child ran off to secure the ingredients, which were then added to the soup. Minutes later, there was another tasting and proclamation of great progress, and the second soldier suggested that "perhaps some carrots would make it even better." A few women went off to collect carrots for the soup, which were then added. Soon after, the third soldier quieted the crowd, tasted the seasoned soup with the carrots, and boldly announced "some cabbage!" Off they ran, men, women and children returning with several beautiful heads of cabbage. And so it went, potatoes and barley and beans piling up next to the pot, awaiting their addition to the wildly anticipated Stone Soup.

A few hours later, the villagers were preparing a long table and breaking out bread and other fine foods in preparation for a village feast. The soldiers were now heroes, and no longer hungry.

The Lesson of Stone Soup

When setting out to start a business, most of us have little more than an idea. In the best case, there might be a team of co-founders, a prototype of the product or service, and perhaps a prospective customer or a few dollars in the bank. Nevertheless, it's still more fantasy than reality, far from being a proven business. There remain missing pieces, or ingredients, and securing them requires an ability to persuade partners, investors and employees of the merits of a venture, and the promise of a worthwhile pay-off. Knowingly or not, many entrepreneurs use the simple notion of Stone Soup, letting people convince themselves of the future potential of a new business.

Let's imagine that you and your partners have written a business plan. You know what it will take to build the business, including cash and other resources that are beyond your personal means – some office space, a small team, and the tools to market and sell your product. You've got a great idea that addresses a known problem that customers are willing to pay to solve, but it hasn't yet been done. Is your solution the right one? Can you actually sell the product? Are you and your partner the right people to build and manage the business? Can you accomplish all of your goals in a reasonable period of time? Before getting started, none of these questions can be answered with certainty. This is where the concept of Stone Soup can help.

One of my earliest ventures provides a real-life example of Stone Soup at work. The approach originated from a pragmatic co-founder and, at the time, it didn't have any name or folk tale attached to it. Our basic problem was simple: being young and relatively inexperienced, we needed credibility for our team and idea. Our solution was to surround ourselves with some of the most highly respected professionals in the field. Of course, this is a circular problem – these experts don't want to risk their reputations by being associated with an unproven start-up venture, and we were just that, a risky, unproven enterprise. This is where my co-founder's suggestion made a difference. His idea was to simply break the cycle by finding a first respected person to support us, and then quickly moving up the ladder until we reached the top people in the field. Up to this point, there were only stones in our soup; now was the time to add our first real ingredients. Within four weeks, we had five of the top names in the field associated with our small, unfunded start-up company. This was well received by investors, and provided enough credibility to transform a high-risk experiment into a successful company.

Stone Soup can be applied to any initiative where the support of other people is valued. It takes advantage of a human tendency to pay attention to trusted friends and colleagues, and to travel in crowds. One must take care with the Stone Soup concept. It serves to pull together resources, or ingredients, that are meaningful for success. If certain people (experts, investors, or partners) believe in an idea, then you want to find them and earn their support as quickly as possible. A note of caution: don't abuse the concept. For example, don't tell one person that another person is interested in your venture when this isn't true. I am aware of a few investment offers that were retracted because an entrepreneur destroyed credibility by telling one investor, for example, that she was talking with another investor – when this was not true. It is not worth the risk to your venture, or reputation – which is without a doubt every entrepreneur's greatest asset.

Stone Soup is not, in and of itself, a means to achieve success. It is, however, a powerful tool that can be used to complement real ideas, real talent, and lots of hard work. If you're on the path to success, trying to make the most of the few resources you have, an appreciation of the merits of Stone Soup can help you to quickly attain ingredients that could make the difference.

Stone Soup to the Rescue

The Stone Soup approach is recommended for most any entrepreneur who is working with limited resources, yet who needs to quickly and effectively build momentum.

This was certainly true for my first serious venture, OncoLogic Biopharmaceuticals Corp. Despite the grand name of the company, we started with little more than an orphan idea. The concept was a brainchild of my two co-founders. At the time, they were both researchers at a respected research institute in Boston. Together, they conceived of the idea that the human body has its own natural (antibody) defenses against cancer. It's a long and complicated story how and why this is the case, but they hypothesized that there exists a certain element of our immune systems that is found in some people, but not others. If we could find this molecule, then we had the beginnings of a possible new treatment for cancer.

The idea was so novel at the time that nobody wanted to believe it. Grant proposals were rejected, and colleagues just smiled and walked away. This is one example where an entrepreneur can make a difference, and why I got involved. The two researchers and I started the venture a few months after we met. We licensed the patent from their institution, each put a few dollars into the company, signed the two of them on as consultants, and began our work. Since there was no money to pursue new research, our first goal was to find an investor – a fairly daunting prospect for our risky, young biotechnology venture with an unproven team and idea.

This is where Stone Soup first came into play. If we were going to get serious with a respected venture capital investor, then we needed credibility for our unproven team and idea. What better way to get this credibility than by formally associating ourselves with some of the biggest and best-known names in the field? If the co-founders, technology, and a thoughtful business plan were the stones (at least in the eyes of our prospective investors), the next few resources needed to be our first real ingredients. First, we spoke with one of the scientists' colleagues, a respected professor at another university. We knew that this individual would like the science and represent it well to others. Furthermore, among this colleague's friends was an especially famous scientist, and we were intent on having him join our Scientific

Advisory Board (SAB). My co-founder's colleague agreed to be a part of the SAB, and then convinced the famous scientist to join us a few weeks later. The soup thickened. From this point forward, things just happened. Armed with two respected SAB members, we quickly signed up a world-class group of scientists to advise us. Others, including investors, began to take notice of our progress.

The best part was that all of our SAB members were true believers in our company's technology. Stone Soup may have contributed to their decision to join us, but they appreciated the science, knew the risks, and accepted our challenge to help by providing advice and support. This was a turning point for our young venture – providing the very credibility we were looking for.

Money would be the next part of the recipe, and having real ingredients in our pot helped us to attract investors. Virtually every investor we contacted agreed to see us. These were not investors desperate to talk to people, but rather some of the leading venture capital firms of the day. Over the course of the next few months, we met with several of them. Predictably, all of them seemed interested but cautious, and no firm wanted to be the first to invest. This is a common problem for ventures with unproven teams (and a problem that is faced not only with venture capital firms, but with smaller investors, as well). We had to overcome this new challenge.

The objective was to get someone to become our "lead" investor and to take the first step that others would then follow. Although we were making progress on this front, things rarely work out as expected. During our talks with these investors, a large biotechnology company got wind of our research and invited us to visit with them. As a result of one of our connections, we were welcomed by the CEO and Chairman of the company, along with other senior people. Within weeks, we had an agreement with a leading biotechnology company. This would prove to be yet another critical ingredient in our ever-evolving Stone Soup – which was quickly becoming a hearty meal.

This agreement provided us with some cash in exchange for the biotechnology company receiving an opportunity to evaluate one of our molecules. In essence, they paid us a healthy sum for the opportunity to "kick the tires" and see what we really had. The agreement stipulated that if they liked what they saw, then we would negotiate for them to buy or license our patent rights. Importantly, this included their promise to share all of their research results with us, something that would prove valuable to us whether or not they decided to proceed with a deal.

The situation provided us with more credibility and cash, adding two more real ingredients to our pot of soup.

At first, things seemed to be going well. The opportunity soon evaporated, though, as the big company ran into financial difficulties a few months later. They decided to depart the cancer therapy field, closed an entire facility and laid off employees. This proved to be the demise of our deal. Fortunately, they kept their word and gave us the data (which was favorable), and we got to keep the cash. Although the future was less certain once again, the ingredients were in the pot and the soup tasted just fine.

At this point, we could have slunk into a depression and given up. Instead, we rallied. The three of us continued to pursue investors and opportunities with a renewed vigor. We ultimately made contact with a venture capital firm that was eager to help. This group introduced us to one of the companies that they had invested in, a well established biotechnology company in the early stages of preparing to go public. Before long, we met with this company, impressed them with our science and team (now credible), and started down the path that led to the acquisition of our young venture soon thereafter.

The concept of Stone Soup enabled us to secure resources one by one, ingredients for our success that may not have otherwise been available. It prompted experts to join us, investors to take note, an established company to agree to a partnership, and ultimately led to our acquisition. The concept of Stone Soup is intended to help a new venture assemble resources by encouraging people to motivate one another. When used properly, Stone Soup provides a powerful tool that can facilitate success.

Chapter 4
Team Building: 10 Rules of Engagement

There is no prescribed order of events for the creation of a new venture. Some entrepreneurs will assemble a team, start a company, write a business plan, and so on. Others will develop an idea, write the business plan, get funding, bring partners into the venture, and so on from there. Although there is no single way to go about it, it is well advised that you consider human capital requirements first, and identify your key team members sooner rather than later. Since people make things happen, getting the right people involved early in the process is best.

There are two major reasons for making the formation of your team a priority. First, the success of any business clearly depends on the people who are doing the work. If a particular position is critical, but a qualified person is unavailable to fill the position, this could even affect the viability of the venture. Second, smart, motivated people, presumably the people you want for your new venture, appreciate the opportunity to contribute to the formation of a business, especially the planning of those activities for which they will be responsible. Although the basic business idea may be yours, their "buy-in" and assistance with refining the initial concept will prove invaluable.

This is not to say that you'll organize all twenty (or two) people expected to get involved with your new venture over the coming year in a single instant, but rather that you need to selectively determine who will be making early contributions and who will act as a partner or co-founder in the "get equity" sense. With whom, if anyone, will you share ownership of the new business? For many ventures, this is not only one of the earliest decisions to be made, but also an important one. The right decision is critical to building a solid foundation.

Marriage may not be the greatest analogy for a business partnership, but you are going to come to know your partners extremely well. Your partners will be a big part of your life throughout your entrepreneurial adventure, so you better be certain that you can live with them – in a closed space, and with a limited supply of fresh air.

Your partners need to be your counterparts. You need to have some large degree of respect for one another, and it helps if you like each other. Successful partnerships also require that participants complement, not compete with, one another. If you're stepping on each other's toes, you won't get past the first dance. While most partnerships can survive or even thrive when things are new, exciting and going well, weak partnerships are prone to fail as soon as challenges (even seemingly small ones) arise.

The key to a truly successful long-term partnership is to choose the right partners in the first place. This ensures the highest probability that things will go well over time, and that you will be able to sleep at night. For example, if one of your partners is responsible for marketing and sales, it is a good idea if she has successfully marketed and sold similar products or services in the past. The same applies to you. A good partnership is like a good marriage: it takes regular commitment and effort to make things go well, day in, day out. Should things turn sour and resentments arise, it's difficult to go back.

Before we consider the characteristics of teams that work, let's frighten ourselves with a few examples of what can happen when things go wrong. I'd recommend that you don't skip this part because while these disasters are common, they are also avoidable. The best bad lesson is the one you never have to learn yourself.

Team Building: 10 Rules of Engagement

One scenario is the enthusiastic entrepreneur, desperate for resources and assistance, who meets an individual desperate to help. One entrepreneur was attempting to start a computer business. We will call him Jim, and his eager new associate Flubby. Flubby is really eager to help because he's just lost his job, thinks that Jim's idea is fantastic, and is convinced that he's going to be Bill Gates to Jim's budding Microsoft. The problem, however, is that 1) Flubby has just lost his job for a very good reason, according to his former employer whom Jim never even bothered to call; 2) Flubby knows very little about the computer business; and 3) Flubby simply isn't Bill Gates. Irrespective of any of this, Jim agrees to proceed with a partnership, inviting Flubby to assume a key position in the now two-person company. Jim provides Flubby with an employment agreement entitling him to some deferred salary, stock according to a vesting agreement (this is an agreement entered into by employees and consultants whereby one's shares of stock are granted, or "vested," over time, or according to certain conditions), and a prominent spot in the business plan. At first, everything seems fine, as Jim is distracted by his many start-up activities. Within a couple of weeks, however, Flubby's incompetence becomes apparent, as does the fact that he has to go. Jim and Flubby agree to part as friends.

Here's what happens next. Flubby calls a month later and asks Jim when he can expect to get paid, and if he can keep his shares. Jim replies, "I'm not sure" and "no," respectively. That afternoon, the assistant to a prominent investor calls to see when Jim and his Vice President of Business Development (Flubby) can come in to speak with him – he is very interested. Finally, Jim gets a call from Flubby's lawyer (his wife's sister's new boyfriend) demanding that Flubby get paid, and also receive his shares because he helped to write the business plan and some of the ideas are his. Since Flubby never bothered to sign his Assignment of Inventions Agreement (another often critical agreement), and Jim never bothered to ask for it, Flubby's issues need to be taken seriously. After consulting with a high priced corporate attorney, Jim hesitantly offers Flubby a separation arrangement that promises to pay Flubby some deferred salary once the money is raised, and provide Flubby with shares of stock representing five percent of the new company. Ouch! In exchange for this, Flubby agrees not to sue the company, or Jim, but this arrangement has yet other devastating effects. First, Jim eventually has the meeting with the investor – without Flubby. It goes well, except when the investor inquires about Flubby. Where is he? What has happened? All of a sudden, the attention is not on Jim's promising new computer venture, but on good old five-percent-Flubby. This raises a series of "red flags" for the investor, and questions such as "how much of my cash will go to pay off Flubby rather than be used to develop the business?" and "is there any chance Flubby could continue to hassle the company despite having signed a Separation Agreement?" The investor notes these issues and politely "passes" on the investment opportunity.

If Flubby represents a nightmare, then Killjoy (another real character whose name has been changed) signifies a nightmare wrapped in litigation, replete with the smell of burning cash. A group of seven technology executives met to plan the launch of a new venture (which is today a successful high-profile company). Killjoy was invited to attend a few of these meetings by one of the co-founders due to Killjoy's expertise in a particular aspect of the start-up venture's technology. The other six co-founders were generally impressed, and informal discussions (and several emails) referenced Killjoy's participation, and the possibility of him joining the team. Killjoy was never actually employed by the venture, or a party to any written contract, although he hung around with several of the co-founders and visited the company's bustling new offices many times. He was never a problem, was occasionally invited to sit in on meetings and offer his advice, and was never given any serious consideration. That is, until the company's planning for its initial public offering (IPO). Around this time, Killjoy let it be known that he clearly considered himself a co-founder of the company and wanted his shares. It turns out that his old college roommate was an up-and-coming litigator at one of the country's largest law firms, and legal action was initiated against the company just prior to its IPO. This happened days before the company would meet with its investment bankers to finalize the pricing of the IPO, a strategic assault well timed by Killjoy's capable attorney. What do you think the company did, considering a $125 million IPO was at risk of delay? Do you think, amidst all the well-planned and well-timed media frenzy that surrounded the IPO, that the company would pause the process, or taint it with a disclosure of litigation? Would they disappoint a dozen investors and more than a hundred employees? Who do you think bore the cost of this oversight? It wasn't the attorneys or investment bankers. It was, of course, the co-founders who should have been careful in the first place by making Killjoy's situation clear, perhaps offering him compensation for whatever services he did perform, and keeping him out of the company's meetings – or else providing him with well-defined consulting agreement.

If you think that either of these situations is uncommon, speak with an experienced corporate attorney or litigator. Employee and shareholder lawsuits happen, and have the serious potential to stop a promising start-up venture in its tracks. The legal costs, perceptions, and headaches can cause partners, employees and investors to turn their backs. Such situations must be avoided at all costs – by being smart about relationships, approaching prospective partners with care, and by having a competent attorney at your side. This last point is especially important; more so when you're partnering with a friend or someone you think you know well. It is often the case that we deal with friends and colleagues somewhat less formally. A good attorney can help us to be sure that partnership or employment agreements are complete, and that every part of an agreement is properly documented. This has the potential to spare everyone a great deal of agony.

Building Your Team: Ten Rules of Engagement

Since the people you choose to work with – the members of your founding team – are your most important asset, and the people who will determine the future of your new venture, it helps to have a few guidelines for their selection. The following factors relate to the building of a team. Keep them in mind as you think about your team and consider your prospective new team members.

- Big Picture
- Competence
- Complementarity
- Structure
- Personality
- Work style
- Motivation
- Shared objectives
- Compensation
- Buy-in

Big Picture: What's the Big Picture, your vision of where you are and where you want to go? It doesn't have to be perfect, but it's got to exist. Your new venture is about to take shape, not by virtue of a 100-page business plan or ideas buried deep in your brain, but by people. Knowing what you want has tremendous value. Such knowledge will be your best guide as you consider other members of your team. Do they fit the Big Picture? Will they be right as the venture evolves and grows? Many otherwise smart entrepreneurs, in their eagerness to "Go! Go! Go!" tend to make poor decisions about partners and employees. This can be a very costly lesson. Take care to determine if a prospective team member truly fits into the Big Picture – not only for the start-up environment of today, but also for the future that you envision.

Competence: This is about an individual not just saying that she can successfully do something, but that she can actually do it. In the corporate world, competence means things like skill, ability, aptitude, proficiency, and an entire breathtaking array of descriptors that result in long resumes. For an entrepreneur, however, the concept of competence is rather simple: can you do it? There are a variety of ways to test for competence, but ultimately it is a judgment call. The reason I say this is because I know too many supposed misfits, whose resumes would not impress the corner variety store manager, who happen to have started and built successful companies. That is not to say that past accomplishments should go unnoticed, but rather that a lack of major accomplishments listed on a resume does not correlate with success or failure in an entrepreneurial environment. It may be irrelevant. Search deeper, and learn all about a prospective employee's or partner's interests, for example. Is she a tri-athlete with several medals to her name? Did he travel around the world, working the restaurant scene to earn his way from one city to the next? Depending on your situation, these may be relevant and impressive accomplishments which, when coupled with factors such as motivation and drive, may indicate a relatively high degree of competence in the entrepreneurial setting. In fact, competence, defined as the ability to actually get things done, is two things: hard factors such as skills and abilities, and soft factors such as focus and determination. Both are required.

Complementarity: Every individual has strengths and weaknesses. For an entrepreneur, an understanding of one's own strengths and weaknesses is beneficial. Based on this information, you can seek team members who not only complement you, but complement one another. This means that you shouldn't involve anyone on your team who simply replicates your skills and abilities, no matter how good the person is otherwise. Focus on people who overcome your (and the team's) weaknesses and round things out. When an entrepreneur clearly recognizes the competencies that he or she lacks, and builds a team to overcome these deficiencies, things tend to work. There's nothing as frustrating as being in a venture with like-minded, similarly skilled and hard working people as oneself, wondering why nothing ever gets done. Sure you've designed and manufactured a great product, but what happens when everyone can build it but nobody can sell it? Think about your venture as a system, like an airplane – you need wings, a tail, an engine, fuel, pilot, etc. Every component plays a role, and even the fifty-cent fuses scattered about a cockpit are critical for the safe and reliable operation of the system as a whole. Be sure you possess all of the critical components, or can comfortably gain access to them, before you take flight.

Structure: Every team member needs to know up from down. An entrepreneurial work environment can be a chaotic place, but competent and complementary team members should have clear roles and responsibilities. If not, teamwork starts to break down. Many entrepreneurs dream of "flat" organizational structures, forgo titles, and treat everyone as equals. That's fine – mutual respect is a wonderful thing – but organizational structure has its place. Everyone should know where they stand, and how they relate to others. Remember our airplane analogy? Suppose that one of our control lines gets momentarily confused, and the passenger seat recliner button for seat 3A decides to talk to the wing? Now suppose that your junior sales person decides to call your manufacturer to change a design feature of your product. And then your senior sales executive decides to take the initiative and correct the situation before you learn about the problem, not realizing that the cost of the correction will bankrupt the entire company. You, along with other members of the team, need to create a clear and useful organizational structure. What are the required positions? Who fills what role? How do these positions relate to one another? Who has authority and takes responsibility for what? Although your organizational structure is likely to be reconsidered and revised over time, start with one. This will prevent or limit confusion by letting people know where they stand as soon as they join the venture, and which way is up. A clear organizational structure speaks volumes about your team and its prospects for success.

Personality: Who is this person? If your first reaction to a person is "he makes my skin crawl," then he probably is not such a good fit. Personality, or the lack thereof, is a necessary consideration. When you start your venture and are working long hours in a tight space, you better like the people you are working with, and they better like one another. That's not to say that everyone will be the best of friends, but compatible personalities are a really good thing. If there's blood on the carpet every time you return to the office, this is a sign of impending doom. Do your best to assess if a new team member brings along a personality that fits well with the rest of the team, and be prepared to act decisively should problems arise after the fact. Get team members involved in hiring decisions as they occur, or at least keep them informed and seek their buy-in. Keeping your current team intact is usually a lot more important than the value of a new team member.

Work style: In some ways, one's work style is a part of one's personality. Some aspects of work style, such as the degree of personal organization (or disorganization), are impossible to change. Other elements, such as preferred work hours, may be malleable. For example, I've worked with many young software developers. For the most part, they sleep late, start work late, and leave work late – and usually make a convincing argument that they can't physically function any other way despite the fact that they can (and do) when it's required. When considering putting together a team, the key is to make sure that such work styles actually fit your venture. If all ten computer programmers work nights, then this particular schedule could work out. If everyone is showing up and leaving at random times, despite putting in long hours, a lack of communication and coordination could ensue. Another work style factor is degree of organization. You might want to explore the ways in which a prospective partner or employee stays organized. If you are someone who expertly arranges the few papers on your clean desk and approaches life with a minimalist attitude, you might find it difficult to work closely with someone who prefers to scatter piles of paper across the floor, and has a desk that doubles as a fire hazard. Work style compatibility is a useful consideration.

Motivation: A prospective team member can love your new venture, have twenty years experience and tons of contacts, but without motivation the person is useless. I am aware of several situations that have failed because an unwary entrepreneur hired a "successful" executive as CEO, or in another critical capacity. Sometimes, prior significant success can equate with satisfaction with one's life, and a reduced drive for additional financial wealth. This makes perfect sense – if someone has put in long hours for the last several decades and now has personal financial security and comfort, why work so hard? Why not spend more time with the grandkids or play more golf? This kind of situation can pose a major problem for an entrepreneurial venture. On the other hand, there are many individuals who are driven by more than financial wealth, and someone with vast experience and success can be the most extraordinary leader or team member – provided that he is motivated. Every team member, from the top down, needs to be motivated to help make your venture a success. In some ways, you will provide the motivation through your enthusiasm, and by creating a meaningful and satisfying work experience. That being said, at least some part of motivation comes from within each individual team member. Take time to confirm that every prospective team member shares your enthusiasm for the venture, as well as your desire to succeed.

Shared objectives: Since you know your Big Picture, and have a sense for the future of your new venture, you now have clear objectives. Objectives come in all shapes and sizes, from "we need to get this done today" to "the company will be public in five years." Team members should be aware of the objectives that relate to them. Everyone should know the Big Picture objectives, as well as the many smaller goals relating to an individual position on the team. Even more important, however, is that each team member shares these aspirations and goals. If you have a vision to accomplish X, and your partner or employee thinks it's better to accomplish Y (and acts on it), then you've got major problems. I was recently involved in a discussion about a possible new CEO for a technology venture. This person sounded great on paper, but when he arrived at our office, one of the first questions I asked him was "what's your vision for the company three to five years from now?" His answer completely opposed that of the company's founder who had spent the last four months wooing him to join the venture. Imagine a team of ten or one hundred people scurrying around, everyone doing what they think is best at the moment, either because they don't know what the objectives are, don't care, or don't support them. Shared objectives for your team are critical for success.

Compensation: The early days of most entrepreneurial ventures typically involve very limited cash resources. In many instances, a founder will invest a few dollars just to pay for a phone line and other essentials, but certainly not enough for anyone to be drawing a fair salary. This makes the subject of compensation a tricky matter for early team members. Many times, early team members will work for deferred compensation. This means that they will accrue a salary, but that it won't get paid until some event in the future (such as a financing), if ever. There are lots of reasons why some entrepreneurs think that people should receive higher-than-usual deferred salaries (i.e. the risk that they may never receive it…); while others think that lower-than-usual deferred salaries are more appropriate. Every employee nevertheless has to be content with his or her entire package. Beyond the base salary, this may include such things as an equity stake in the venture (stock or options), a commission or bonus based on performance, an employment agreement providing certain benefits and/or assurances, or a specific title. Take care to affirm that a team member is content with his or her package. There are two problems that can arise, and both can be prevented with advance thought. The first is real, and the second is perceived (and quickly becomes real). The real problem arises when a new team member accepts a package without any comment and is immediately disappointed. Although the disappointment may not surface for some time, it eventually will. It is better to prevent this up front, by making sure that one's compensation is both fair and agreeable, or by distancing yourself from anyone who insists on compensation that is excessive. Second, your team can become immediately and totally disgruntled by a common perceived problem. Suppose that somebody gets a really sweet deal. Then suppose that everybody else learns about this (which you should consider inevitable even if all of the details are not disclosed). What do you think happens next? Everyone gets upset with you, and the situation could back you into a corner. Do you think that the single employee with the great deal will voluntarily agree to give it up, to the possible satisfaction of every other team member? Not likely. The reality is that every other team member is going to come kicking and screaming to your office to demand a pay raise or more equity, or else he or she will sit and work quietly and perform poorly, all the while circulating resumes to your competitors using your company's computers. When it comes to compensation packages, whether for partners or employees, be fair, be consistent, and assume that nothing will stay completely confidential despite your best efforts.

Buy-in: Last but not least, get buy-in from your existing team. There's nothing as divisive as a new employee who walks in and immediately offends everyone, and nothing as gratifying as an interested team that contributes to its own destiny. Involve others in the team building process.

Your team is your biggest asset. The quality of your team is also the best predictor of your company's success. Take the time to carefully select your team members.

Chapter 5
Your Lawyer as Superhero

The right business attorney can be the difference between life and death for your new venture. This is not some hysterical exaggeration, but a fundamental truth about life for an entrepreneur. While some people consider a lawyer a necessary evil, you will want to consider your attorney an essential ally in the entrepreneurial process.

In some ways, a business is simply a web of relationships. These relationships include those you have with your co-founders, employees, customers, suppliers, professional service providers, investors, and many others. While you are ultimately responsible for determining the nature and details of these relationships, your attorney should first be able to advise you (about what you might expect in a term sheet or lease, for example), and then be able to clearly document the details of each relationship. While many attorneys can do the first part reasonably well, the second part demands a great deal of skill and experience.

The following few pages describe five real-life examples of my experiences with various attorneys and their firms (first three bad; last two good). Some details have been changed to protect the innocent. This is then followed by a list of characteristics that will help you to identify an attorney that is likely to be right for you.

In one of my early ventures, I was under the delusion that we should be represented by one of the city's "top tier" business law firms. Huge mistake, but one that is shared with many first-time entrepreneurs. I was under the impression that bigger is better and that high cost somehow relates to high quality and access to a firm's connections. Through one of our local venture forums, I came across a firm that proclaimed to have an extensive practice focused on new ventures. I contacted one of the partners at this firm and met with him. Our legal needs were not dramatic, just a couple of very simple filings for our incorporation, documents to issue shares to a few co-founders, and other minor agreements (when I use the term "minor," I do not mean unimportant, but instead agreements that are rather standard and would be based on templates). This firm agreed to work with us on a deferred fee basis, like many firms do, meaning that we would pay the firm's bill when we received our initial round of funding. For most law firms, common business documents are not drafted from scratch, but developed from a template or form. I did not know this early in my career, but I sensed that this might be the case when the draft documents that we received from this prestigious firm contained another local company's name and contact information. A high-priced junior associate had filled our company's information into the header of each document and then ever so efficiently overlooked the fact that he needed to revise several details elsewhere – a process that eventually took more than a few additional hours of billable time (according to the associate). Being naïve at the time, I worked with the associate to correct and revise the documents to reflect the particular needs of our new company. A few months later, I received an invoice for more than the average house was worth, most of which was due to the associate's sloppiness. After a month of haggling with the partner, he begrudgingly adjusted the bill to a realistic level, and also was kind enough to recall our agreement about the bill being deferred until we received some funding. In my experience, this partner's (and associate's) belligerent attitude and poor ethics are more the rule than the exception. My personal opinion is that, in general, big firms best serve large clients.

This next true story is about an attorney who wore a handkerchief in his suit pocket the size of which rivaled the flag that hangs over our nation's capitol building. He was considered an expert in a certain area of the law, and we needed just such an expert. He ever so kindly agreed to meet with me to discuss our company and project, not to offer any advice, but to describe his firm's capabilities and costs – exactly what I would expect from a half-hour introductory meeting. We spent less than thirty minutes together, and I was actually impressed and considering using his firm. Then, about two weeks later, I received a bill for our brief meeting! I called him as he was leaving for one of his numerous holiday parties, and he actually said to me, "I was expecting your call because I thought you might have a problem with the bill – I'll take care of it." I never quite understood this behavior, and I never approached him or his firm again.

Years later, I experienced yet another big firm debacle. I needed a patent attorney with expertise in medical devices. Through a trusted friend, I was introduced to a patent attorney at a well-known law firm. The project was fairly straightforward (preparing and filing a simple patent application based on input from our team) and I wanted to know the bottom line cost. Sitting down at dinner, she told me that the maximum bill to get the patent filed in a timely manner would be a specific amount. I agreed to the amount and deadline, and we started work. The one lawyer capable of actually writing the patent then promptly disappeared to Europe for a month to work with a large client. Our project was then passed around from one associate to the next like a hot potato, while the partner supposedly supervised by cell phone. One associate was knowledgeable enough that we agreed to work with him. A few weeks later, we received an invoice for about three times the agreed-on maximum amount, despite the fact that the patent application had not even yet been filed. We found another law firm the next day and filed the patent application soon thereafter. I sent the first firm a reasonable check (for the originally agreed amount less the cost of having the second firm file the patent application) and noted that it was "payment in full for all services rendered to date," and stated that the check would be canceled a week later unless deposited. They cashed the check and never wasted my time again.

Here's a summary of the several mistakes that I made:

- I believed that bigger would be better
- I was a small client lost inside a large firm
- I allowed associates to learn at my expense
- I didn't confirm a cost limitation in writing
- I expected only a high ethical standard
- I sought prestige over substance

As you begin your own quest for the right lawyer, know that most big law firms thrive on their relationships with large corporate clients and sometimes use small clients as training fodder for inexperienced associates. All of this makes sense since large clients have vast legal needs and pay big legal bills, all necessary if a large firm wishes to stay in business. Furthermore, associates stay late and do a lot of the heavy lifting. Although most great corporate attorneys were once associates, often at large law firms, I generally prefer that associates do not touch my work – unless they are handpicked, well supervised, and billed at reasonable rates. The reason for this last point is that although many firms suggest that associates are cheaper and therefore beneficial to smaller clients, the reality is that associates take longer than an experienced partner to complete most tasks. In the end, it's a wash financially, so I'd prefer that the work get done by a senior attorney or partner – unless it's a fairly simple matter.

Now let's fast-forward to sunnier days. Superman (this is how our founding team actually referred to him) is the managing partner at a medium-sized business law firm in Boston. He saved our venture's life at least a few times. Superman knows how to get things done, as he's been around the block quite a few times. For example, when investors balked at our valuation, Superman stepped in and told us "take the valuation since it's more than what you expected last week, and without it the venture will be dead in the water." He then helped us negotiate several details that proved to be even more important than the valuation in the long-run. Superman is an attorney's attorney, the kind of professional who could (and did) explain the finer points of securities law to other lawyers without offending them or blowing up a deal in the process. He has both the power and the touch.

Since your company's counsel is such a critical part of your venture's life, including personal access, proximity is important. So when I relocated, I searched far and wide for another Superman. I found Superman II in a Boston-suburb outpost of a large California-based law firm. This satellite office has a lot of pluses, most significantly that it has the feel of a medium-size firm, yet retains access to big firm resources. They have a high partner-to-associate ratio, meaning that all of their associates are handpicked and work closely with a specific partner. Also, this firm's exclusive focus is on emerging companies. To date, I have started two new ventures with Superman II. He has all of the characteristics that I've learned to look for.

What are these characteristics? In summary, this is what your Superman (or woman) should bring to the table:

- Focus – does a few things very well
- Experience – seen it all before
- Competence – work done right the first time
- Accessibility – promptly returns calls/emails
- Connected – knows lots of helpful people
- Reasonable cost – bills are fair and honest

Despite the problems that I've encountered with some of the larger firms that I've worked with, the selection of an attorney should be focused on the individual, with the firm's resources, use of associates, and billing practices taken into consideration. Let's take a closer look at the characteristics that define the kind of lawyer you want to work with:

Focus: When was the last time you said, "Gee, I think I'll go on down to the hardware-donut-carpet store for some coffee"? Or, "my general practice physician would like to conduct the heart transplant – he's never done it before and he thinks it would be fun to do one on me before he retires." Likewise, don't use a general practice lawyer, or any other non-business attorney, for specialized business counsel. This is especially true for any start-up venture, which demands a great deal of focused expertise in order to build a solid foundation. Your lawyer needs to practice areas of law that are relevant to you as an entrepreneur, and not have distractions that make him or her less of an expert in these areas. Although focus is a hard quality to determine, it can be assessed by learning if an attorney practices in lots of other areas, such as real estate law (many "business" lawyers also do this, which often takes up more of their time than does the "business" part of a practice), or general law (such as family law, estates, etc.). For example, since my ventures often involve technology, receive external financing, and are intended to be sold to other companies, I seek to work with an attorney who focuses on legal organizational issues, private financings, securities law, and mergers and acquisitions. Both of my Supermen are partners at law firms that are exclusively focused on business law, are expert in all of the areas I have identified as critical to my ventures, and have direct access to partners focused on related areas of the law such as technology transfer, real estate and taxation.

Experience: In addition to being focused, your attorney should be experienced. I expect to pay a premium for experience. I want an attorney who advises me based on years of experience with hundreds of clients, not just a dozen start-ups that he or she has handled over the past several years as an associate at a large law firm. In fact, it is preferable that your lawyer not only have experience with lots of clients, but that he or she has experience working in various firms and/or legal environments.

Experience is not just quantitative, but also qualitative. A lawyer can spend many years at a large firm, even have partner status, and yet be completely ignorant of the most basic entrepreneurial issues. There are quite a few respected "corporate" attorneys doing million (or billion) dollar deals who could not recite the details of a venture capital terms sheet. Do not be swept away by tall tales or superhuman feats. Be sure that your attorney is regularly doing the kind of work that your business will require. Check references and be sure to confirm that an attorney has experience relating to the issues that you expect to face. For most entrepreneurs, these issues are:

- New venture structure
- Founder agreements
- Employment agreements
- Investment strategy/terms
- Financing documentation
- Guidance for negotiations
- General contract law

Additionally, you may require access to specialization in:

- Tax law
- Real estate law
- Employment law
- Mergers & acquisitions
- Strategic partnerships
- Intellectual property
- Technology transfer
- Public securities law

If you find an individual who fits most of your criteria, but whose experience is limited in some way, explore his or her firm. Are there partners who make up for a lack of experience in a particular area of the law? Not everyone can have vast experience and know everything, yet every attorney should know his or her limitations, and where to access the necessary resources. For example, Superman would refer me to one of his partners for tax law counsel, and another for employment law advice. Superman II has a close working relationship with one of his partners who is an expert in intellectual property matters and license agreements. I regard these relationships and expanded capabilities as a strength, and as a sign of intelligence and focus since one individual can't possibly be an expert in everything, especially in such a complex field as the law.

Competence: Competence is the ability to properly get things done. Keep in mind that it is possible that a lawyer can be focused and experienced, yet lack competence. The profession includes many types of people, and some seem more concerned with image than substance. Take substance over image any day. Both of the lawyers that I have mentioned previously, although successful partners at successful firms, do not dress in expensive suits or spend a lot of time marketing themselves. In fact, neither of their firms advertises widely, unlike many large firms that need to keep up appearances. If a firm embroiders its logo on the fine linen that arrives with the coffee, then you're in the wrong place. Run past the Renoir, down the elevator, and out the appropriately revolving door.

Competence is about doing things right the first time. It's about capability, skill, aptitude and also proficiency. You know it when you see it, but since you will need to find a competent attorney before you begin the relationship, here are a few thoughts. First, don't fall for a fancy office or other signs of the try-too-hard-to-demonstrate-success syndrome. If an attorney is dressed to the nines, using an expensive pen, acting like an ass, then you probably can't afford him. If she doesn't appear to grasp your business, then you probably don't want her. And if this individual seems like he doesn't need you, then you don't need him. Second, look around and use common sense. Does this person treat you with respect? How do they treat their colleagues, including the secretaries? Your attorney will represent you and your business, and may play a role in your relationships with investors and business partners. You need for this individual to represent you in the best possible light and to be capable of advancing (rather than detracting from) various relationships. This is the softer side of on-the-job competence. For purposes of your new venture, a great lawyer should not only be a legal expert, but also have some socially redeeming features.

Accessibility: When you first made contact, how was your call or email handled? How quickly was it returned? A prompt reply is not necessarily indicative of future responsiveness, but getting a return call two weeks later is a blatant sign that you're not going to be a priority or get prompt service. When you meet an attorney for the first time, ask the following questions:

- Do you travel often?
- Do you answer your own phone?
- If not, do you have a dedicated assistant?
- How long does it take for you to return a call?

- Do you use email and attachments? (some firms even have secure online document access)
- Do you give clients your cell phone number?
- What's the turnaround time on a simple document, like articles of incorporation or an employment offer letter?
- What work do you do? What work is done by the associates, if any? Who are the associates, if any, that you work with? (Then meet them.)

I expect a return phone call or email either later the same day or by the end of the following day, even if it is a call or email from an assistant telling me that the attorney is traveling. I also expect to have a cell phone number for an emergency, although I've only once had to resort to a weekend business call. I do my best to be respectful of the fact that my attorney has other clients and priorities, and a personal life. I want to be sure that my needs are a priority when they need to be. It is common to use email, and you should expect a reply within a day or two, at most, depending on the urgency of a matter. While I don't expect a complex document to be turned around in an instant, I do want to know where things stand, and also seek to rest assured that progress is being made. As a client, your experience should improve over time. Very few of your requests will need immediate attention, but it is always helpful to have good access to your lawyer.

Connected: Is your lawyer well connected in the business community? How extensive are his or her relationships with colleagues, investors, and others? Such relationships may prove invaluable to you as an entrepreneur. First, being well connected helps to confirm that an attorney is well regarded by others. Second, it could open doors and make a tremendous difference to your success.

Your attorney should be your business partner. As such, he or she should not only be able, but also willing, to make introductions. If your lawyer doesn't believe in you or your venture, then he or she shouldn't be representing you. In some circumstances, such as getting a meeting with a prominent venture capital firm, it is necessary to either personally know someone at the firm, or else to be introduced by a credible source. A respected attorney can help in this regard. This can prove crucial to a start-up venture. Although larger firms will claim to have lots of connections, you should confirm that specific connections that are important to you will be made available to you.

Be respectful of your lawyer's connections. Don't ask him to send your business plan to every investor he knows.

Your lawyer would be stupid to do this – and you would be foolish to ask. Remain focused on your needs, and maintain realistic expectations. Don't get excited just because your lawyer knows Warren Buffet or the number one venture capital firm in the field. In fact, take care to make the most of the few introductions that your lawyer does arrange for you; otherwise you will quickly learn that all future connections are simply "not interested".

Reasonable Cost: A pricey lawyer or firm, or aggressive billing practices, can cripple an entrepreneur and stop a venture in its tracks. Even if the invoices are deferred until funding occurs, an outrageous bill is a problem. For example, an investor may become discouraged if she is informed that 20% of her investment will have to go to pay past legal expenses, rather than to build the business. (Of course, if such a situation arises, negotiate a fair payment plan acceptable to both the law firm and the investor.) Also, investors may view excessive legal bills as indicative of past legal problems, or an entrepreneur who isn't able to manage expenses. This is why it is so important to keep all of your company's expenses under control, irrespective of when they need to get paid.

Reasonable cost should be evaluated in two ways. First, what are the billing rates and expected cost of services?

An experienced lawyer and reputable firm should be able to provide you with some guidelines, although this is likely to be a range. Also, how will the firm invoice you? Will the firm expect to get paid immediately for its work, within a defined period of time, or will it defer your bill until the venture is financed?

Deferred billing is a common practice. It typically means that invoices will be sent to you, but that they do not need to be paid until some pre-negotiated time or event in the future. It is important to determine exactly what "deferred" means. For example, suppose the lawyer says that you can pay once the venture gets funded. Well, what exactly does "funded" mean? Does this mean the first dollar, the first instance that there are sufficient funds to pay the legal bills, or a pre-specified minimum amount of money? Also, you need to clearly learn what happens if the venture does not get funded. Are bills forgiven, or will you, as the entrepreneur, have partial or full personal responsibility to pay them. I recommend that you do your homework, consider your law firm as you would a potential investor, impress them, and get the following deal: 100% deferral of legal fees (except for out-of-pocket expenses which will be pre-approved by you if above a certain amount) until the venture gets funded at a minimum level of $Z (which depends on the particulars of your venture). Finally, the company is the client, and you bear no personal liability for the fees, or else there is a pre-established upper limit. This type of arrangement will assure that your firm is not just racking up hourly fees, but 1) truly believes in you and your new venture, and 2) will do everything possible to help you get funded so that they can get paid. If your new venture does not need external funding, you might ask for billing concessions in the beginning, or simply start paying the bills and establishing a long-term relationship. (Keep in mind that "your" law firm will represent your business and not you personally. Often, this is not a problem, such as when you own a majority of a business. In other situations, however, you are well advised to be sure that you have a lawyer advising you personally.)

The importance of having a qualified attorney represent your business cannot be overstated. This individual will represent you and your new venture, and his or her work will either prevent (or enable) innumerable problems in the future. This person, in the best case, can make the difference between the success and failure of your new venture, by placing your venture on solid legal ground, helping you to facilitate relationships, documenting these relationships, and contributing a legal perspective to an entire range of important business decisions. Although the cost of quality legal service can be high, the value of exceptional advice should never be underestimated. Your lawyer should be an essential member of your team, and a resource for information that is vital to your success.

Chapter 6
The Business Plan and Beyond

Have you ever been to the Louvre, or any other great museum for that matter? Consider that each masterpiece has taken its creator perhaps hundreds or thousands of hours to create, yet the average museum visitor will spend only moments staring at it. Leonardo da Vinci's Portrait of Mona Lisa – such a nice smile!

Your business plan is likely to resemble just another masterpiece hanging on a long-forgotten wall in a grand museum, assuming that it even gets hung. Imagine that each visitor is an investor or other interested party – very few will stand and gawk, the vast majority will stare for a moment and then move on, and several will run right past everything, through the museum and out the door, just to say that they've been there.

Almost nobody thoroughly reads a business plan. It's a rare exception that anyone will pay much attention to the document, except for the people who wrote it. In my experience, the more prominent the reader, the less time he or she will even hold your plan. The real value of a business plan is to i) enable you and your team to all be thinking along the same lines, and ii) serve as a calling card that encourages some action from a recipient.

I should note a few exceptions to the rule that "nobody reads a business plan." First, it should certainly be read and understood by the people who wrote it, including every founder and key team member. It will be an instant circus if, for example, during an investor meeting one co-founder says something different from the next. Second, some people are paid to screen business plans for a living, usually by investment firms, and a few of these individuals will take the time to read through an entire plan that is of interest. For every 100 plans an investor receives, one to ten of them might be reviewed in detail. Finally, some investors really do read plans, especially individual investors with time on their hands. All of this assumes, however, that a venture is worthy of being considered, and the plan proves worthy of being read. The moment a reader thinks otherwise, a business plan is likely to be sent straight to the recycle bin.

If only a few people read the plan, then what use is it? Why invest the time and effort to write one? The business plan, although often misunderstood, has a significant three-fold purpose:

1. **It's a right of passage:** If you cannot write your ideas down on paper, or feel that you don't have the time to do so, you significantly decrease your chances of success. Thinking and then writing it down is a valuable exercise. It's not about filling pages with empty words, but rather clearly and concisely organizing and presenting your ideas in a way that best represents you and your venture.

2. **It's your masterpiece:** This might sound corny, but it's true. Your business plan embodies and presents your team's talent, skills, abilities, and personality – as well as its weaknesses, fallacies, ignorance and stupidity. Michelangelo's David may have taken him hundreds of hours to sculpt, and the masses will stand in front of it for fewer than sixty seconds apiece, but it's a big part of what represents him – what he's known for. In this way, your business plan represents you. If the plan is good enough, it gets hung on the wall and occasionally studied by someone who may truly

appreciate it. The bottom line is that a business plan represents you when you can't be there to represent yourself. The majority of people will not read it in its entirety, but will look at it, perhaps read a few lines here and there – and generate their entire initial impression of you in this way. It is critical that this first impression take you in the right direction – closer to your objectives. In many cases, the goal of a business plan is simply to facilitate an in-person meeting with the recipient.

3. **It can open doors:** The business plan can open doors and get you places, or it can mock and torment you. In the best case, a business plan is useful as an oversized calling card. If your lawyer or accountant sends it along to a prospective investor, it will introduce you in your absence and hopefully entice an investor to want to meet with you in person. On the other hand, a business plan with sloppy appearance, lack of substance or poor spelling will produce great misery for you. More than once I have seen hardened executives torn to shreds with their very own words by an overzealous "vulture" capitalist intent on making an example of them. At minimum you want to be

certain that your business plan doesn't get in the way of your goals – it needs to support them.

As the reader of several hundred business plans, I can tell a lot about a person and their venture after spending about five minutes with a plan. Its design tells me about personality; its writing style and vocabulary tell me a lot about education and intelligence; the structure of a plan tells me about one's organization and understanding of the "Big Picture," as well as the priorities of a particular venture; the substance of a plan unveils knowledge and expertise; certain details suggest prior experience as an entrepreneur or executive. Even the physical appearance of a business plan can convey useful information.

For example, one afternoon I received (by courier service) a leather-bound plan for a new software venture. Within minutes, the guts of the plan were in the trash and the nice leather binder was sitting on my shelf. At the other end of the spectrum, I am familiar with a handful of ordinary-appearing business plans that have received compliments from several hardcore investors even prior to their meeting the entrepreneurs. This is a good sign, not because the plan means anything much, but because these investors actually think that they know and like the entrepreneurs and their new venture before they've even met. You want this to be the case for you.

In general, successful business plans appear simple, yet are deceptively substantive. They inform a reader clearly and concisely. These business plans are written on a level that respects readers, yet elevates them by engagingly introducing new information – details that transform a readers' knowledge into excitement. If your business plan accomplishes this, you are off to a very good start.

Expectations for a Solid Business Plan

A solid business plan represents the team that is starting the business. As such, a business plan is expected to be unique – while conforming to certain "soft" and "hard" expectations. Soft expectations include common sense items such as good writing and careful organization. Soft expectations permeate your entire document, and are obvious at first glance. If the plan is poorly printed and hastily stapled together, then it is unlikely that much attention has been given to other details such as spelling and substance. If the entrepreneur does not really care, then why should the reader? Hard expectations are the content elements that a business plan generally includes, like the sections of a plan and information they contain. There are no hard and fast rules here, although most plans do contain most or all of the hard elements that are described later in this chapter.

When considering the expectations for your plan, you should think about the expectations of your audience. Ask yourself the following two questions:

- Who is my audience?
- What do they expect?

Identifying your audience is critical. For most business plans, the audience will be a certain type of investor, such as a venture firm, individual investor, or bank. Each of these investors has unique expectations. Investors are not, however, the only audience. Your plan could be for internal use, for review by employees, or for presentation to prospective business partners or service providers. In fact, most business plans (or portions of them) are seen and used by more than one audience.

When considering your readers, anticipate their needs. Write at their level, speak to their current knowledge, complement and extend their understanding. You're not going to get far by describing an industry to an investor who is already an expert in the industry. In fact, if you do this, you're only likely to state something that he or she does not quite agree with, which will guarantee an early end to an otherwise promising relationship. What are their expectations not only for your business, but also for the document that represents it? Think about what the audience wants, what they are looking for – problems they perceive and how you can solve them. Your reply, in the form of your business plan, must address these problems head-on, without distraction. If you accomplish this, then your plan is likely to keep a reader's attention and lead to the next step – a meeting or conversation. In fact, the goal is almost always to bring about some action or next step. Never forget this as you write and present your business plan. Keep your goal clearly in mind – and write your plan as a means to a well-defined next step.

Soft Expectations for a Business Plan

How many times have you judged a book by its cover? The "cover" is one of the many soft expectations that will cause your business plan to stand out. Although every plan requires substance in order for the document to be taken seriously, it first needs to be taken – seen and also appreciated before a single word of it is read. While hard expectations encompass the substance of any business plan, soft expectations include all of the physical and psychological attributes that make the substance shine. Whether they'll admit it or not, most investors and other readers appreciate both the steak and the sizzle.

Appearance/Design: One of the first things that a reader will often do is to "flip through" your business plan. The reader wants to get a feel for the plan, and importantly, determine whether or not it is worthy of being read in detail. Appearance matters. That's not to say that some unattractive plans haven't gotten the attention of serious investors, or conversely that spending lots of money on design, paper and binding make a favorable impression, but rather to suggest that the average plan would benefit from some TLC. Take a few simple steps to create a document that is representative of the type of venture you are proposing, and make it readable. First, include design elements, such as a nice logo, or a little color. Some pictures really are worth a thousand words (others are not). Be consistent with your design, font, type sizes, and headers throughout the plan. Use graphics when appropriate, but don't overuse them – i.e. when they don't convey useful information. Make the plan readable. Is the font easy on the eyes? A serif font is usually best, and don't use reverse print or ALL CAPS (studies show that words in capital letters are harder to read). Use page numbers and a table of contents. Some technical business plans even include a glossary. I also recommend a nice looking cover, and binding that permits the plan to be opened flat on a desk and to be readily copied. Print the plan on good paper, perhaps something with slightly more weight than the usual copy paper. Don't overdo it, but create a document that is visually appealing. Also, since more and more business plans are delivered and read electronically, be certain that the electronic version retains all of the attributes of the hard copy document.

Organization: The structure of your plan will convey something about the structure of your brain. Are you organized? Do you see things clearly and have your priorities in proper order? A well-organized business plan, including a table of contents and section headings (and sub-section headings, if useful), is prerequisite for a good first impression. Also, try to tell a story with your plan. There should be a natural flow to your plan, a logical progression of information that causes a reader to be drawn in, and to learn and become convinced of the merits of your new venture.

Substance: There's got to be meat on the bone, or the intelligent reader will never bite. Your plan should be full of substance, never opinion or fluff. Specific suggestions for the type of substance (i.e. sections of your plan) are provided in the next section. In terms of the form of the substance, take care with declarative statements. Instead of saying that the market is large, use data. Rather than provide general facts, stay focused on information that is relevant to your venture. Stay away from wild adjectives and the like – which raise warning flags for investors. For example, instead of saying that the "market is extremely large and growing at a fast rate," say that the "market is $120 million in the U.S. and is growing at a rate of 32.6% per year, according to ABC Market Research." The more specific and credible the information, the better.

Spelling, Grammar and Vocabulary: Invest the time to press the "spell check" button on your computer, and to have your plan proofread by someone who passed sixth grade English. Also, unnecessary big words are a waste of perfectly good letters. Recent studies indicate that the use of smaller (common English) words leads readers to believe that the writer has a higher intelligence. Never attempt to write in a style that isn't your own.

Personality: If proper grammar and spelling are basic to good writing, giving your business plan "personality" has the potential to transform it into something great.

Although your business plan is sure to contain many facts and details, give the reader a reason to want to continue to read the document – to turn the page. Even better, make them want to read it by providing a degree of entertainment alongside all the valuable information. Express yourself in a way that lets each reader know who you are – that you are not just an expert at Szvelt-Kerr Algorithms or counting beans – but that you possess a personality and that meeting with you and possibly also working with you would be worthwhile and enjoyable.

Delivery: There's nothing as sad as a beautiful business plan, representing a great team and opportunity, getting ignored because it got mangled in the mail (perhaps the email equivalent is when your email gets filtered into a bulk mail folder and deleted without ever being read). I don't mean to suggest that your business plan needs to be delivered by Federal Express or similar means, which is unlikely to impress even the receptionist who signs for it, but rather that you take reasonable care in its handling, packaging and ultimate delivery. If you're going to mail your business plan, use a stiff outer envelope, such as those available from several couriers, including the U.S. Postal Service. A reliable delivery service will insure the plan's timely arrival and help you to determine the best moment for follow-up contact. It is also common to send a business plan as an email attachment. This method is preferred by many investors since it allows them to read it on the go, as well as forward copies to associates. If you are going to distribute your document in electronic form, however, take care to stabilize it so that your audience will see what you intend for them to see. Many word-processed documents can appear different when they are opened using another software application, or different version of the same software. Fonts, margins and page breaks could get altered, transforming a once beautiful document into a mess. If possible, convert the document to a standard file format such as a PDF. This will provide you with control over its appearance, and also limit a recipient's ability to alter any of the content.

Hard Expectations for a Business Plan

The following is a list of some elements that you should consider including in your business plan. Again, every plan is unique, so keep your audience in mind, and use your best judgment as to their expectations and how you will best meet them. If possible, look at some successful business plans as examples (it's also helpful to see some unsuccessful business plans as an example of what not to do). Your lawyer, accountant or banker should be able to share a few non-confidential plans with you, and there are several examples available in books and on the web. Try to learn which ones actually got funded, and the real stories behind them. It does not do you much good to be looking at business plans without knowing which ones succeeded and which ones failed, and why.

Executive Summary: This is usually the first section of a business plan. The Executive Summary needs to be hard-hitting. Every sentence needs to command attention and provide useful information. If your audience cannot figure out what you do by the end of the first paragraph, then the entire document is going into the trash. The Executive Summary needs to sell your venture, and fast. It must excite the reader in an intelligent way, without deception or exaggeration. Take care to include all of the information a reader expects. What is the problem or need that your new business is addressing? What is your solution? Why is the venture so wonderful relative to the competition? Who are you? Why should a reader believe that your team can execute the plan and make money? How will the investor make money? The goal of the executive summary is simple: to convince the reader to take the next step. Explicitly state the next step. What are you trying to accomplish? For example, state that the venture is seeking a specified amount of financing and that the reader should contact you for more information about the investment opportunity. Finally, it's useful if an Executive Summary provides not only an introduction to the rest of your business plan, but can also act as a stand-alone document. The stand-alone version is useful when you want to either interest an investor without overburdening them with the complete plan, or when you want to send something, but don't want to give the recipient all of your plans and specific details. I will often email an executive summary, which usually leads to a request for the full plan. If someone asks for something, they are more likely to take interest once it's received.

Market/Problem: For readers who actually get past the Executive Summary, this is one of the most important sections (along with the team biographies). This is a place to shine, to make the unequivocal case that your market is not only large and growing (relative to the ambitions of your venture), but also desperate for your company to solve a problem that nobody else is solving. Invoke hard facts gathered from credible third-party sources. Describe the market. What is the need in the market? Quantify the need. How much is a solution to the particular problem worth to the market? What will customers pay? Prove it. How does all of this translate into potential sales revenue for your company? Also, who are your competitors and what are their strengths and weaknesses? Research your market extensively, and present the relevant information in a logical manner, rather than a recitation of one fact after the next. Your readers will truly appreciate this.

Product/Solution: If there is a need that isn't being met, and your business is prepared to meet that need, then you may have a legitimate business. The next step is to introduce your product or service – your solution to the problem that was presented in the Executive Summary and validated in your market overview. Tell the reader what you intend to sell to the target market. Provide some details, including designs, schematics, drawings or photographs. If you have a prototype or actual product, make this known. If it's a service, describe it in detail – how does it work? What are your solution's features, advantages, and benefits? In this section, you need to explain not only why your solution solves the problem, but also why it does so in a way that's better than the competition. If you're already selling a product or service, include customer testimonials. If necessary, how will you protect your product or service? Do you have patents? Does the product or service rely on your team's unique expertise, or can it be replicated? Or perhaps you have special ties to your customers? By the end of this section, a reader should know 1) what you plan to make, market and sell, 2) how your product or service stands out in relation to the competition, and 3) the most compelling reasons why customers will buy your product or service rather than somebody else's.

Business Model: This part of your plan describes how your business is designed to make money. The term "business model" refers to the process by which your product or service is going to be made, marketed, sold and distributed – and how the process translates into profit. It's helpful to demonstrate that you have a model that makes the most sense for your industry, product or service, targeted customers, and the resources that you're working with. Take a reader through the various aspects of your business model. Focus on the areas where your company is unique. Describe how your model works so that a reader understands how you are going to produce the product or service, market it to your target market, and generate revenue and profitability. For example, if you're selling muffins, one business model would be to make the muffins in a home kitchen in small batches and then sell them exclusively through a website – customers could place their orders online and you'd ship them out. A seemingly similar business model, but one that may actually be more costly and complex, would be making the muffins in a home kitchen in small batches and then selling (and delivering) them to retail stores. A different business model for a muffin manufacturing business may involve establishing a commercial kitchen, hiring a sales team, and marketing and selling the muffins to retailers and restaurants nationally. Other variations on the theme might involve using contract manufacturers to make the muffins, or independent sales reps rather than an internal sales force. In any case, a business model will clearly state how a business is designed to make money, and it will usually answer the following questions:

- What exactly is the product or service?

- How will your product be manufactured, or the service get delivered?
    o Internally made/delivered
    o Use of third-party contractors
    o Buying/importing it
    o Combination of these
    o Other

- Who are your actual customers?
    o Individual consumers
    o Retailers
    o Wholesalers
    o Manufacturers

- o Combination of these
- o Other

- How will the product or service be sold
  - o Internal sales force (i.e., you)
  - o Dedicated sales representatives
  - o Independent sales representatives
  - o Your company's website
  - o Somebody else's website
  - o Your company' catalog
  - o Somebody else's catalog
  - o Combination of these
  - o Other

Every business model should be viable – achievable with resources that are either at hand, or within reach. In this section of the business plan, your goal is to convince the reader that your business model makes sense, and that it is realistic and achievable. Your business model is likely to evolve over time, but you need to start somewhere.

Team: When I read a business plan, this is the very first section that I turn to – before the Executive Summary. I want to know who wrote the plan, and why the team is qualified to be starting the business. Each team member biography should stick to the facts. Never exaggerate, yet highlight the parts of each individual's biography that support his or her role in the venture. Each biographic profile should be narrative and run from about a third of a page to no more than a page. The presentation can be enhanced by including photos of each individual (a nice touch that I don't see too often). If you decide to use resumes instead of narrative biographical sketches, take time to make sure that all of the resumes are similarly formatted. If your team members have lengthy resumes, such as scientific or technical CVs, consider using brief narrative biographies in the body of your plan along with inclusion of complete resumes in an appendix.

Financials: Although people other than investors may read your business plan, most readers will want to see some financial information. I can't tell you how many times I've seen business plans that have contained either 1) no financials at all, or 2) fifty pages of spreadsheets with numbers legible only with the aid of a magnifying glass. One common mistake is the "10-Year Financial Projection." When's the last time you knew what you'd be doing next month, let alone ten years from now? You need to strike a balance. For many businesses, financials projected over three to five years will do the trick. Also, don't get creative with your financials – use a standard format that an accountant would normally use and that can be found in any reputable book on the subject. If you don't have a thorough knowledge of accounting, don't fret – read the next chapter on cash flow. It will give you an overview of the most important accounting concept for a start-up entrepreneur. Develop and include a cash flow model for your business. This will go a long way to inform an investor about how much money you need, how the cash will be spent, and how and when the investment will be paid back. You will ultimately need other financial statements – a balance sheet and profit and loss statement – but the cash flow statement is the most informative and provides a great place to start.

Appendices: During the creation of your business plan you will collect other information that you may want to share with investors. This information could include: detailed resumes, market research, product designs and photographs, real estate plans or site maps, competitor information, marketing literature, patents, publications, press coverage, etc. While some of this information may be appropriate for the body of the business plan, most of it is best left for an appendix. If extensive, supporting documents can be included in a second binder.

The Business Plan and Beyond

A Note on Business Plan Software and Services

There are several software products that claim to help you with the writing of a business plan or virtually write it for you. Some of these provide testimonials like "I purchased this software on Monday and got $5.0 million in venture capital financing on Friday!" What they fail to mention, even those software products with somewhat more realistic claims, is that they can generate red flags for investors. There's only so much customization that a piece of software can provide, and this risks producing a plan that is not a true reflection of you or your venture. In some instances, such software (or portions of it) may be helpful, but take care in its purchase and use, and never fall for unrealistic claims. The same holds true for business plan writing services, or consultants, who claim to be able to write a plan for you. These people are most likely writers who may know something about business, but it's doubtful that they are experienced, successful entrepreneurs who just happen to love to write. No matter how tempting their claims or inexpensive their services (you generally get what you pay for), it's your reputation and future that are on the line. Do you really want to place your destiny in anyone else's hands?

That being said, some tools exist that could be helpful. There are several excellent books on business plans, some of these tailored to specific types of businesses. Also, all of the leading accounting software programs include tools to help you build the financial statements that you'll need. An investment in an appropriate software package (some of these are excellent and relatively inexpensive) could be wise since you'll need it sooner or later.

Beyond the Business Plan

Once you have poured everything you have into creating your business plan, it can feel like it's not getting the attention that it deserves. Too many entrepreneurs place too much emphasis on the plan. Yes, it's important to have one – a necessity for most of us. Also, it's nice if it is well written and also well received. That being said, the business plan is not your business. More than anything else, you and your partners are your business, and you and your partners are going to succeed only by building relationships with others. A business plan can facilitate this, but it is up to you to find your audience, deliver the document into the right hands, follow up, and persuade others that they should help you to reach your goals.

Chapter 7
Cash Flow 101: From Bathtub to Boardroom

Cash is the fuel of every new business venture, and every entrepreneur should have an intuitive understanding of the concept of cash flow. Cash flow entails how dollars move into, and out from, a business over periods of time. For most businesses, it's the ultimate indicator of success, and an understanding of cash flow is an important skill for finding your way to profit and success.

Every day, month, or year, cash flows into a business in a variety of ways, including revenue from sales of products and services, as well as any money that investors invest in the business. Likewise, every day, month, or year, cash also flows out of a business in a variety of ways, such as payments to employees, suppliers, landlords, investors, the government (e.g., taxes), and many others. At the end of each period, a certain amount of cash is hopefully left over. Whatever is left over at the end of any one period is the amount that is available at the start of the next period.

Sounds simple, and it is, although there are executives of large companies who seemingly fail to grasp the concept. An intuitive understanding of cash flow is so simple that there is certainly no need to complicate the basic concept. As such, I'll use a simple analogy to explain it: a bathtub.

A bathtub is a nice model for cash flow. Water flows in through the faucet like cash flowing into a business, and water flows out through the drain like cash flowing out of a business. Depending on the relative speed of the water flowing in and out, water either accumulates in the tub or runs out. If the water is flowing in faster than it's flowing out, the water level rises. If the water is flowing out faster than it's coming in, the water level goes down and eventually the tub goes empty. It's that simple.

For most every business, the goal is to be sure that, on average, water flows into the tub faster than it flows out, and that the tub never runs dry.

From Lemons to Lemonade

Let's explore the concept of cash flow using the bathtub model, and take a look at a day in the life of Henry's Lemonade Empire – a fictional business run by a young entrepreneur. While a lemonade stand could be thought of as a relatively simple enterprise, it nevertheless serves us well as we gain an understanding of cash flow.

First, let's review the three relevant parts of any tub. The faucet lets the water in. The drain lets the water out. The tub itself holds the water. In the drawings that follow, a drop of water below the faucet indicates that the water is flowing through the faucet into the tub. A drop of water near the drain indicates that water is flowing out through the drain and out of the tub. A dotted line shows where the water was before the described event. A solid line shows where the water ends up after the described event. The final water level for any given event is the same as the starting water level for the very next event.

Here's a sample tub:

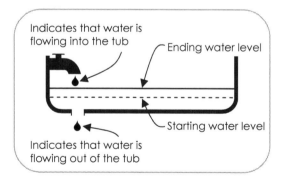

A Day in the Life of Henry's Lemonade Empire

Saturday 5:00 a.m.

Henry wakes up well before the sun rises. He's excited to start setting up for the day's business. At this moment, possibly because most of the world is still asleep, there is no flow of water in or out of the tub. Henry is starting the day with no money at all – the tub is empty.

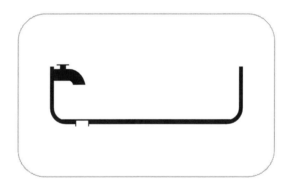

>>>

Saturday 5:30 a.m.

Henry is thinking about all of the supplies that he needs to buy for the day, including lemons, sugar, cups and ice. He makes a shopping list, and then wakes his parents at 5:30 a.m. on the dot. In their stupor, they agree to LOAN Henry $20 to get the business off to a start.

$$
\begin{aligned}
&\$0 \quad &\text{Starting amount} \\
&+\$20 \quad &\text{Loan from parents} \\
&=\$20 \quad &\text{Ending amount}
\end{aligned}
$$

The tub fills with $20.

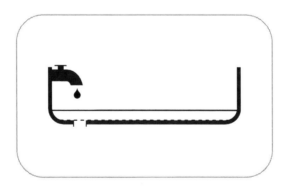

>>>

Saturday 5:40 a.m.

Henry wants to be sure he's set up in time for Saturday morning customers. He gets on his bike and heads out to the local grocery store. He purchases everything that he needs for $15, and remembers to gets $5 in small change. At this point, he's got lots of supplies, and the tub is now down to $5 in cash. Remember that we're focused on the cash situation only, and not non-cash assets.

$$\begin{array}{ll} \$20 & \text{Starting amount} \\ -\ \$15 & \text{Cost of supplies} \\ \hline =\ \$5 & \text{Ending amount} \end{array}$$

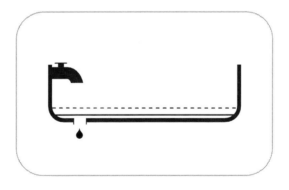

>>>

Saturday 6:30 a.m.

Henry quickly sets up his lemonade stand along the bike path and starts making lemonade for his customers. He plans to sell each cup for $1. If he's lucky, he thinks that he'll be able to sell 50 cups today for a total of $50. The first customer comes along and buys one cup for $1. The level in the tub rises by $1 to $6.

$$
\begin{array}{ll}
\$5 & \text{Starting amount} \\
\underline{+\,\$1} & \text{Sale (1 cup)} \\
=\$6 & \text{Ending amount}
\end{array}
$$

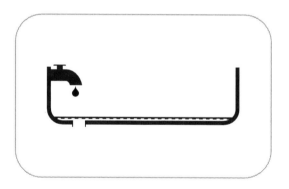

Saturday 6:47 a.m.

Minutes later, a family drives by, stops, and buys 4 cups of Henry's lemonade. Things are going well and Henry is confident that he'll sell lots more. He's already sold $5 worth ($1 a few minutes ago and $4 now), and his cash is up to $10 so far – the $5 cash that was in the tub after he purchased the supplies *plus* the $5 in sales revenue.

$6	Starting amount
+ $4	Sale (4 more cups)
= $10	Ending amount

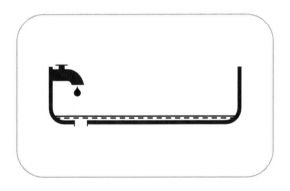

Cash Flow 101: From Bathtub to Boardroom

Saturday 12:00 p.m.

By noon, Henry has sold 20 more cups, for a grand total of 25 cups sold and $25 in sales revenue. This amount, along with the $5 in change that he started with, fills the tub with $30 in cash. And the day is just heating up…

$10	Starting amount
+ $20	Sales (20 more cups)
= $30	Ending amount

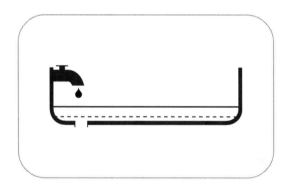

Saturday 1:22 p.m.

Of course, nothing goes perfectly, and a crazed biker has veered off the path and ruined one of Henry's signs. He's in need of a new sign, but he doesn't want to close shop just to make another one. He decides to hire his younger sister Jenny to create a new sign. After some negotiation, Henry finally agrees to pay his sister Jenny $5 to make the new sign. The tub goes down by $5 to $25.

$30	Starting amount
- $5	Paid to Jenny for new sign
= $25	Ending amount

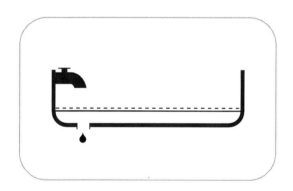

>>>

Saturday 4:00 p.m.

Fortunately for Henry, the rest of the afternoon goes well, and he sells out (another 25 cups). All 50 cups of lemonade have been sold! The tub is full with $50 in cash: $50 from the sale of 50 cups of lemonade, plus the $5 that he started with, less the $5 that he paid for the new sign.

$25	Starting amount
+ $25	Sales (25 more cups)
= $50	Ending amount

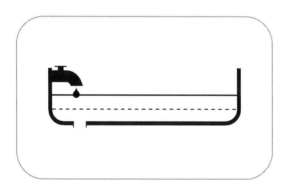

Saturday 5:00 p.m.

Henry packs up his lemonade stand and returns home for dinner after a long day of work. He finds his parents and pays them back the $20 that they loaned to him in the morning. He still has $30, his profit for the day, which he plans to use to buy more lemons and other supplies in order to make even more money tomorrow!

$$\begin{array}{ll} \$50 & \text{Starting amount} \\ \underline{-\ \$20} & \text{Loan paid off to parents} \\ =\$30 & \text{Ending amount} \end{array}$$

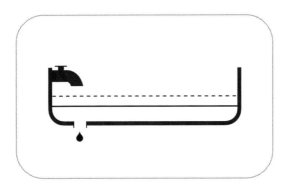

Cash Flow 101: From Bathtub to Boardroom

A Quick Review

Cash flow is simply the flow of cash into, and out from, a business – providing an understanding of:

1. How much cash is in the business at any given moment in time, and;

2. The health of the business – whether it is making or losing money over time

When cash is flowing in faster than it's flowing out, on average, a business is doing well – it's accumulating cash.

Beyond the Basics

The bathtub model allows us to take things another step, and to anticipate a few complexities and opportunities. One complexity is that lots of things can happen at once. It is fairly typical, for example, to be making cash sales (inflows) and paying bills (outflows) all in the same day. The critical realization is that things don't really happen all at once – keep the bathtub model in mind and picture things happening one step at a time.

There are also several opportunities that become clear when we use the bathtub model. Many businesses time inflows and outflows so as not to run out of cash. For example, it pays to fill the tub as quickly as possible, and empty it as slowly as possible. Along these lines, most businesses will encourage their customers to pay for their purchases as soon as possible, while the same businesses will take their time paying their own bills.

Unless you're a mathematical genius who is able to keep a running tab in your head, you will need some tools to help with all of this – a computer and some accounting software are best. I use two tools: a spreadsheet program and accounting software, both of which are available and reasonably easy to learn how to use.

Real Cash Flow Analysis

The bathtub metaphor is intended to help provide an intuitive understanding of cash flow. In many instances, however, you will want to take it one step further, and try to estimate (or project) the cash flow of your venture before actually diving into it. A projected cash flow is a very important tool for an entrepreneur. This financial statement is best learned by looking at examples, and also finding a good book dedicated to the topic. Keep in mind that the concept is very simple, however the actual projected cash flow statement can become complex. I use a spreadsheet program (Microsoft Excel™) to create cash flow projections. Accounting software (including Intuit QuickBooks Pro™) is suggested for keeping books once a business is operational. Since many accountants use this software, it makes it easy to share information with them. This saves time especially during tax season.

A Few Words about Your Accountant

Alongside your lawyer, your accountant will play an important role in guiding your success. Whereas most of your lawyer's activities will focus on relationships that will extend into the future (partners, investors, suppliers, customers government, etc.), most of the work performed by your accountant will focus on documenting your past activities, as well as helping to plan your financial future. This includes review and reconciliation of your books, preparation and filing of tax returns, and assistance with budgeting and financial planning – especially your cash flow statement. Additionally, a good accountant can help you with financial record keeping, permitting you to:

1. Accurately record your company's finances
2. Understand and project your financial situation
3. Minimize taxes and maximize your income

Find an accountant who communicates clearly, gets work done in a timely manner, and bills you reasonably. An accountant's role can vary tremendously. While some businesses "check in" with an accountant only during tax season, other ventures seek an accounting professional to serve as an integral part of the founding team, even to act as a part-time Chief Financial Officer (CFO). In fact, there are many individual accountants and small accounting firms that offer to serve as "part-time CFO's," and work closely with entrepreneurial companies.

Most accountants are focused on their profession and stay up-to-date with the tax code and other accounting standards. Hire an accountant who takes her profession seriously. Like your lawyer, you'll want your accountant to help keep your business on track, and to make you a smarter entrepreneur.

Chapter 8
Five Fun Things to Do with Your Lawyer

Now that you have found a lawyer, and perhaps have a team and completed business plan, it's time to really get to work. There are formalities that need to be taken care of in order to legally establish your company, define the various relationships between each team member and the company, and secure financing and other resources.

Before getting started and meeting with your attorney, it will benefit you to have a grasp of the concepts involved. Keep in mind that the following pages do not provide an exhaustive analysis or legal advice, but will prepare you for a discussion with your co-founders and lawyer. There are five key issues that you'll need to address:

1. Establishing the new venture as a legal entity
2. Getting a firm grasp on how equity is issued
3. Creating an ownership structure and deciding on equity allocation among early team members

4. Determining how each individual relates to the company – employee, consultant, etc.
5. Preparing for the future: getting things lined up for investment and operations

1. Establishing the Legal Entity

I find that many first-time entrepreneurs obsess over this step. Although there are several considerations relating to which form of entity to use, and quite a bit of fact and opinion surrounding the choice, don't get bogged down in the process. If you have a reasonably clear vision of the future for your new venture, and a good attorney, you'll be able to make the right decision.

There are four major types of legal entities:

- Sole proprietorship
- Partnership
- Corporation
- Limited Liability Company

As an overview, 70% of all businesses in the U.S. exist as sole proprietorships. Corporations and limited liability companies represent 20% of all entities, and partnerships make up the rest – less than 10%. When adjusted for size, the corporate structure reigns as the most important.

The following paragraphs contain general descriptions of each of the four types of entity. Please keep in mind that corporate and tax laws change over time, and only your attorney can advise and guide you. Nevertheless, it helps to have a basic understanding.

Sole proprietorship: As its name clearly implies, a sole proprietorship is a business owned by one person. The company exists by name only, such as Joe's Plumbing Service, which is really Joe. It is formalized by filing a "Doing Business As" (DBA) document in the city or town where the business is located. A sole proprietorship is the simplest and least costly entity to form and manage since it takes little effort to establish one, and maintaining it requires virtually no additional effort beyond keeping good records and filing your personal tax returns. It is best for very small enterprises that have minimal liability issues (potential to get sued, etc.) and that do not require investment from third-party funding sources. To be clear, a sole proprietorship means you – you and your venture are one and the same. If your company gets sued, you are actually the one getting sued. There is no barrier between you (meaning your personal assets) and the company like there is in a corporation or limited liability company (LLC). On balance, a sole proprietorship is a good option for any single-owner, single-employee business with no liability concerns and no need for outside investment.

Partnership: If two or more people operate a business, they can form a partnership. Actually, if you are working with one or more partners and have not incorporated, you have formed a partnership in the eyes of the law. Before describing a partnership as a legal form of entity, my opinion is that the LLC has surpassed the partnership in a few respects (the LLC is described in detail below). In fact, an observer will note that many law firms that were previously partnerships in the past are now legally organized as LLCs. In any case, a partnership is a form of legal entity created when two or more people decide to go into business together. It doesn't technically require a written partnership agreement, although there does need to be a common understanding about the arrangement (known as a "meeting of the minds"). A partnership has a few characteristics of note. First, it can work well for smaller companies with multiple owners, especially for professional service firms. Second, it can be less costly to form (versus a corporation or LLC), but the reality is that the expense is relatively close. Another benefit is that taxes are passed on to the individual partners and not taxed at the partnership level (no double taxation as is the case with most corporations) One large downside is that each partner is personally liable for the actions of her other partners. A misstep of one of your partners could cost you personally. Personal assts are not protected from creditors, and while somebody else may have caused the liability, you could personally end up paying for it. While partnerships can be formed with just one type of partner (general) to create a General Partnership (GP), or two types of partners (general and limited) to create a Limited Partnership (LP), general partners are the ones involved in the operation of the business and will always be held accountable. LPs are used to limit the liability of certain non-operating partners such as investors – the limited partners. The bottom line is that the partnership has lost some of its luster due to the LLC. It should be compared to the LLC (and corporation) and considered only when partners are known and trusted, and also when overall liability concerns are minimal. Finally, most investors shy away from funding partnerships, and venture capital funds (most set up as LPs themselves) cannot invest in them due to the tax flow-through nature of the entity.

Corporation: The word corporation is derived from the Latin word *corpus*, meaning body – a corporation being considered a body of its own. It is a distinct entity that is owned by its stockholders. Stockholders of a corporation (of which there may be one or many) elect a board of directors (consisting of one or more members). The board of directors hires the Chief Executive Officer who runs the day-to-day operation of the business, including hiring and firing employees. Since a corporation is a distinct entity, all business is transacted with the corporation, and not with its individual employees. The corporation enters into many different kinds of relationships, with people as well as other companies. It has its own tax identification number and bank accounts, and is responsible for its own liabilities – which are not the personal responsibility of its directors, officers or stockholders (except in instances of fraud, etc.). This liability barrier is a major benefit of the corporate entity. Another major benefit is its ability to accommodate outside investment from a wide range of sources, including angels, venture capital funds, and also banks. A corporation can have one or more classes of stock. For example, founders may hold common shares and investors may own Series A Preferred stock. This can be important in certain kinds of financing transactions, especially with venture capital investors. The corporate structure is also flexible, relatively cost-effective, and can accommodate nearly all business models. The downside, however, is a corporation's shareholders are taxed twice on profits. First, a dollar of profit is taxed at the corporate level. Then, when funds are distributed to a shareholder as a dividend, this is taxed again as personal income. (Such "double" taxation is the subject of debate, and tax laws change, so check with your lawyer or accountant). In certain situations, such as a family-owned corporation, it may be possible to bypass double taxation by paying oneself extra salary or a bonus (rather than a dividend), both of which are generally only taxed at the personal level since they would be expensed by the corporation. Another possibility for corporations owned by a small number of shareholders is to file an "S" election with the IRS. This permits income to flow through to the personal level, but may have other disadvantages such as limiting the number of shareholders. Many corporations do not pay dividends, but rather reinvest their profits back into the business – with the hope of advancing the business, growing its value, and selling the entire corporation at some point in the future. A corporation is sold when all of its stock is transferred to the new owner(s). The sale of stock is treated as a long-term capital gain and taxed at a lower rate, so long as the stock has been owned for more than a year. Of course, by the time you read this, tax rules may have changed, so be sure to consult an expert. The bottom line is that a corporation typically involves tax considerations that are less favorable than other forms of entity, but is clearly preferred for companies intended to be financed by venture capital and other sophisticated investors. Overall, a corporation should be considered by most entrepreneurs as a possible form of entity, especially when it is desired to protect personal assets, and when a business is likely to be funded with venture capital.

Limited Liability Company: A limited liability company is like a cross between a partnership and a corporation. The LLC, while its documentation and nomenclature are different from that of a corporation, retains most of the major benefits of a corporation, except that its taxation is treated like a partnership – whereby taxable income is passed along to the individual owners (not taxed twice). As mentioned in a previous section, the LLC is used by many law firms and it's a good bet that it was invented by lawyers (for lawyers) – so you know that it's got to be good. The owners of a LLC are called *members*, as in *we are members of the club*. The club is operated according to a document called an Operating Agreement, which can be very complex. Laws for LLCs, like those for corporations, are determined by each state. As such, the rules vary somewhat state by state. In most instances, the downside of a LLC includes limitations on the number of members and the inability of most venture capital funds to invest due to their own legal/tax constraints. That being said, if your investors are individuals, then it may be prudent to start your venture as a LLC. The LLC is especially useful for companies that are investing in research or product development since investors can take tax losses during the development period. Of course, a LLC is also good if you are making money, since taxable income is only taxed at the personal level. A LLC is also an excellent choice of legal entity for service partnerships (law firm, consulting practice), as well as any multi-owner business that is intent on securing funding from sources other than venture capital funds – or that is financed by its owners.

As one might expect, each form of entity has advantages and disadvantages. The decision depends on your goals, liability concerns, likely investors, and whether or not the company is intended to generate dividends or be sold to the public at some point in the future. Here are a few guidelines for discussion with your attorney:

- If you are on your own, want to start small, and seek to minimize costs and legal filing headaches, then a sole proprietorship might be the right way to go. You should consider liability issues, and the means of protecting yourself, such as insurance. A sole proprietorship can be transformed into a corporation or LLC at some point in the future, so it may be the fastest and most cost-effective way to get a business off the ground.

- At the other end of the spectrum, if you know that you'll be pursuing venture capital funding from firms or other institutional investors, then it is a virtual requirement that you be incorporated as a "C" corporation. Although you can incorporate in any state, most venture capital-backed businesses incorporate in Delaware. A few of the reasons for this are that the State of Delaware offers several useful benefits relating to corporate governance, liability protections for officers and directors, and well-established case law.

- In the middle, if you require outside investment but expect it to come from individual investors, then the LLC could be your best bet, although an S corporation might also be considered.

The most challenging decision is when you realize that your business is going to require external funding, but you don't know where it is going to come from: venture capital, angel investors, or possibly even a loan from the bank. Although most individual investors will invest in a C corporation, especially when venture capital financing is anticipated, the tax benefits offered by a Subchapter S Corporation or LLC can be appealing. If such uncertainty exists, you are going to need to make some assumptions and work with your attorney to make a final decision.

2. How Equity is Issued

It's a good idea to review how a corporation issues shares of stock, since many ventures will be incorporated, and many first-time entrepreneurs do not understand how equity is actually issued (the same general principles can be applied to a LLC or partnership). Here's how it works. First, a corporation "authorizes" a certain number of its shares when it files its articles of incorporation. This is an arbitrary number, and could be 1 or 99 or 1,000,000,000. Most companies will authorize a relatively large number of shares since it doesn't cost more (in most states), and to make the number easier to divide up. The corporation then "issues" some of these shares. For example, let's say that your new venture authorizes 1,000,000 shares. There are four equal co-founders, and the corporation decides to issue 50 shares to each individual co-founder, each person thereby holding a 25% stake in the company (50 shares per person divided by a total of 200 issued shares). The decision to issue the 50 shares (or any number such that the total number of shares issued to all four founders doesn't exceed the total of 1,000,000 authorized shares) is an arbitrary one, as well. The number could just as easily be 100 shares each, 1,000 shares each, or 250,000 shares each. The reason that you may want to avoid issuing 250,000 shares to each of the four founders in this case is because you want to "reserve" some authorized shares for issuance in the future, possibly to an investor or your future employees. Although you can increase the number of authorized shares by filing an amendment to your articles of incorporation in the future, it is advisable to plan ahead and issue a portion of the initially authorized shares – leaving the remaining authorized shares set aside for issuance in the future.

Next, let's assume that you decide to take on a fifth co-founder on equal terms. To accomplish this, you would simply issue another 50 shares to this new person (these "new" shares come from the pool of "authorized but not issued" shares), increasing the total number of "issued and outstanding" shares – the number of shares actually held by shareholders – from 200 to 250. Each individual's 50 shares now represent a 20% stake in the company (this reduction from 25% to 20% each is called "dilution"). It is important to note that the original co-founders do not "give away" any of the shares that they already own – in other words, their issued shares do not get redistributed. Instead, the corporation issues additional shares from its pool of remaining authorized shares.

It is important to note that dilution of one's ownership *percentage* does not necessarily equate with any dilution in *value* – it may, or it may not. This is a critical point, and a lack of clear understanding about this issue can lead to unnecessary debate, or worse. For example, let's say the fifth partner is a very senior professional, the equivalent of a star athlete, someone who will bring new customers to your venture. You believe that this will increase the overall value of your company by 50% - she will bring in lots more business, and all five partners will share in the increased profits. Once the 50 shares are issued to your newest partner, although you own a smaller percentage (a 20% stake, versus the 25% stake that you previously owned), the actual value of your shares is increased.

Here's why: If prior to the fifth partner the company was worth $100, and after the fifth partner joins the company it is worth $150 (a 50% increase in the value due to her credibility, contacts, etc.), and your old 25% stake is now reduced to 20% (keep in mind that it's still 50 shares), the old value of your shares was $25 (25% of $100), while the new value is $30 (20% of $150). Work through the math for yourself and never forget this concept – it's all about building the *value* of your shares, which has little to do with maintaining any given percent ownership.

One counter argument that I hear when co-founders are contemplating a transaction that involves issuing shares to investors or new team members is "I don't want to lose control of my company." I can only offer this humbling advice: control of a successful company has more to do with one's usefulness and contributions to the venture, rather than the percent of shares held. If you act like a fool, despite the fact that you own 51% or more of the company, you will be challenged at every turn, possibly even by your investors and their lawyers. Alternatively, I've seen small minority shareholders (and even highly competent individuals who own no equity at all) control companies by virtue of their intelligence, credibility, and overall value to the success of the business.

Continuing with our example, let's bring on an investor. Suppose that an investor wants to invest $1 million for a 50% stake in the company (recall that the company has 250 shares issued and outstanding before an investment). Following negotiations, you would accept the investor's money and issue her 250 shares of the corporation's stock. These 250 shares come from the pool of authorized (but not yet issued) shares and they represent 50% of a new total of 500 shares that are now issued and outstanding. Your 50 shares would be worth $200,000 on paper (an oversimplified upper estimate that does not consider a wide range of details). This value is based on the fact that an investor paid $1,000,000 for half the company, giving the business a paper valuation of $2,000,000 ($1,000,000 divided by 50%). Since you and your partners each own 50 shares, which now represent a 10% stake for each of the five of you, your personal shares are worth $200,000 (the $2,000,000 value of the company times 10%). There are many variations and complications in reality (such as investors having certain preferences – special rights and privileges that are described in the financing documents), but this is the general manner in which a corporation's equity is issued and valued.

Let's take a look at two concepts that are important if you have partners or expect financing from outside equity investors: vesting and cliffs.

- The term "vesting" refers to one's right to get (or else keep, depending on how the arrangement is legally structured) shares. Vesting usually occurs over a period of time to encourage an employee to stay with a company, although shares can vest for other reasons. For example, the phrase "straight-line quarterly vesting over four years" means that one receives one-sixteenth of his promised shares every three months for four years – there being 16 quarters in the four year period – provided that the individual remains with the company. Vesting is usually "straight-line", meaning that an equal number of shares vests at regular intervals, most often monthly or quarterly, for a period of 3-4 years, although 1-5 years is not unusual in special situations. Also, vesting is very often accelerated (sped up) in certain situations, such as when a company is acquired. Vesting is generally used to motivate founders and other employees (anyone getting stock) to remain committed and involved – so that an individual won't just take their stock and disappear once the company is funded. Most investors will require that all key employees have vesting agreements, although the specific vesting terms are usually negotiable. Vesting indicates a person's commitment to a venture, so take care to structure a sensible vesting arrangement.

- Another term that is used in association with vesting is "cliff." A cliff is a fixed period of time that one is required to be involved with a venture before he gets the first allocation of shares subject to a vesting agreement. For example, "four year straight line monthly vesting with a one year cliff" means that the person would get one forty-eighth of his shares as each month goes by – there being 48 months in the four year period – except that this person would not receive the first year's worth of shares until the first anniversary of his involvement with the venture (the "cliff"). This is done to incentivize a key team member to remain with a venture for at least the first year.

- In practice, some portion of shares is most often vested on day one, and the remaining shares vest following a cliff. For example, if a founder is set to receive 1,000,000 shares of stock in a new venture, he might receive 10% up front (fully vested – his to keep forevermore), and the balance of 900,000 shares would vest periodically over a certain number of months or years. Furthermore, he may have to remain involved with the venture for at least a certain period of time (the cliff) in order to receive the first portion of vested shares. Twelve months is a reasonable period of time for a cliff. Vesting accelerates if the company is acquired, or if his employment is terminated without cause.

Once shares vest, nobody can take them away, although there will be limitations on the sale of the shares. If the founder leaves the venture voluntarily, or is fired for cause, he forfeits all of his unvested shares. This is one possible vesting arrangement for a key team member.

One footnote relating to shares in a start-up company is that the shares are private, not public. In other words, although each stock certificate represents an ownership interest in a company, its owner cannot sell the shares on a stock exchange. Only shares of public companies can be freely sold. Depending on one's particular situation, it may be possible to sell shares in a private transaction. There are legal restrictions on the sale (and purchase) of equity in private companies, and companies themselves often further restrict these private transactions.

The legal process of transforming private shares to public shares is called an initial public offering (IPO). An IPO is a mechanism whereby a company registers its shares with the Securities and Exchange Commission (SEC). It's a complex and costly process, and one that should only be attempted by a team of professionals. An IPO enables a company to sell its shares to the public. This is a key event for many companies since it 1) allows the company to raise money by selling new shares to the public, and 2) lets founders and investors sell their shares to the public (often after a waiting period). If you are the founder of a company and hold a bunch of vested shares, then this is your opportunity to transform your paper shares into cash – by selling them to the public. The IPO is the way many high-profile entrepreneurs have become rich. (In reality, the riches of many of the wealthiest entrepreneurs are tied up in their companies. They often sell some of their shares, or take loans against them, but nevertheless their fortunes rise and fall with a company's stock price.)

Another way for shareholders to transform their shares into cash is by selling a company for either cash, or else in exchange for public securities (shares that can then be sold on a public stock exchange). This occurs when all of the shares of a company are acquired by another entity in a private transaction, rather than sold to the public using a public offering. Private sales of entrepreneurial ventures are much more common than taking a company public.

Acquisitions and IPOs are referred to as "exit strategies" by professional investors since they allow investors to "exit" an investment – hopefully with more cash than they invested into a company in the first place. Keep in mind that relatively few companies seek an exit strategy such as an acquisition or IPO. Most entrepreneurs will actually seek to own a profitable business that provides regular paychecks to its employees, and repays investors by paying off loans or issuing dividends. In essence, most businesses ultimately provide an ongoing exit strategy rather than a big pay-off that occurs all at once. The form of exit strategy is correlated with the type of business, and also its investor. For example, venture capitalists will almost always strive for an IPO, and revert to the sale of a company to another (larger) company if an IPO cannot be pursued or completed for any of a variety of reasons.

3. Deciding Who Should Get What

The previous section provides an overview of how equity is issued, and how it gets transformed into cash. Now it's time to determine how equity in your company will be distributed to the individual team members – the actual number of shares each team member will receive, as well as any special provisions as to how he or she will receive the shares. "Who should get what" is a discussion to be had by you and your partners, although your attorney can play a role by contributing thoughtful advice and helping to settle any disputes that may arise. In fact, the "who should get what" conversation is usually one of the most challenging aspects of the start-up process. This is disturbing, because it shouldn't be for two reasons. First, if anyone quibbles over small amounts of equity, as is often the case, then this person doesn't understand start-up dynamics. Every time I hear a founder state that he deserves an extra percent (when he's being offered 20%, for example), I know that he is inexperienced, or worse. Second, legal structure of your venture, including vesting agreements, obviates most of the reasons that people get worked up in the first place. Your lawyer can provide a major contribution to your understanding of equity, what it means and what it doesn't mean, and the real issues that should be productively discussed and agreed on.

Although equity distribution is uneven in many instances (you get 90%; I receive 10%), these situations are usually relatively simple to negotiate and agree on. For example, if you start a company and use some of my ideas (but I will otherwise have no obligation to the company), I may agree that a 10% stake in the venture is a fair offer since you're doing all the work and my ideas are only a small part of the overall business. At worst, I may negotiate within some range, but it would be absurd to think that I should receive 90% of the shares when you are going to be doing all of the work. Although every situation really is unique, looking to past "comparable" deals is helpful.

Problems arise when things are more closely matched, like when three similarly successful people come together to start a company. In this case, there is not likely to be a clear justification for any particular equity split. Nobody knows the future, who will ultimately contribute the most value to a venture, so the "I'm more important than you are" argument is useless. It's crucial to work to not let ego interfere with the entire future of a new venture. If founders are closely matched, the damage one can do arguing about why he or she deserves a bigger piece of the pie than anyone else is purely destructive.

Two take-home messages:

- *Understand the real value of equity*: The focus is on the word "value." Don't forget that a share is only a piece of paper that represents a certain value. Think about it this way: you start out by receiving a certain number of shares. This number may vest over time, but assuming that you expect to stick with the venture, you'll end up with this number of shares. The number of your shares might grow a little in certain instances, but what you start out with is likely to be quite close to what you end up with. In other words, more or less, your number of shares is fixed. Next, think about what you can do with this share certificate. You can hang it on the wall or use it as toilet paper. Don't ever forget that it's just a piece of paper. Your real interest, of course, is its value. What will it be worth when you sell it? How many dollars will you ultimately get for it? Value is determined in only one way: multiply your fixed number of shares by the price per share. This will give you the value. Note that since your number of shares is fixed, the price per share is what makes all the difference. Therefore, focus on the price per share – increasing it with every decision. This includes an early decision to be fair and reasonable with your future business partners. Jeopardizing relationships early on can have lasting effects, and can cost you dearly.

Equal ownership could be the answer, especially when the differences in value that founders offer are small, and the potential cost of dissatisfaction over equity exceeds this value. Here's why:

- o   Everybody is in the same boat
- o   There is a sense of mutual respect
- o   Nobody has the upper hand equity-wise
- o   Everyone will work hard for the venture

o   The approach is simple

- *Understand the real value of people*: As an extension to the ideas presented above, keep in mind that the right partners are expected to make valuable contributions to *your* personal financial success by applying their talents, aspirations and connections in a way that will grow the value of the venture as a whole. If you take steps to undermine a person's dedication to the venture, whether or not this individual reacts openly, then you are destroying value. Think about the absurdity of getting a few extra percentage points of the initial equity in a venture, only to have a co-founder hold a grudge, or worse – to leave six months later with stock in hand. Keep the Big Picture in mind. Be decisive about whether you want to work with someone in the first place. Do not send mixed messages by including an individual as a part of a team only to insult them with an inferior offer. The only result will be that you undermine the success of your venture before it even gets off the ground. Your co-founders are a critical part of your success. Choose them well and then treat them well.

A practical note: when one or more founders decide to contribute cash, in addition to their time and energy, it is useful to separate the two. For example, first discuss and issue equity as if everyone was contributing only his or her time and energy as a team member. Next, determine a reasonable value for the equity (i.e. price per share), and have each of the cash contributors (co-founders, seed investors, etc.) buy shares at the established price. This removes cash as a complicating factor, and enables all co-founders to invest on fair and equal terms – at founding and subsequently. Alternatively, it is not even necessary to establish a valuation if you use convertible notes – one means of financing that is described in the next chapter.

4. Personal Agreements

Just because you own shares in a company doesn't mean that you have any other relationship with the company. This means that you now need to consider how you and your co-founders will interact with the new company. It's helpful to place each person into one of three categories:

- Employee
- Consultant
- Advisor

Employee: An employee, whether part-time or full-time, expects to receive salary and typically benefits from the company. Although such compensation may not be paid right away, it's part of the contract, and one of several issues that you will need to discuss with your lawyer regarding each employee. Other topics include:

- Are there any issues that could complicate an employee's status? For example, are there non-compete agreements that have been signed with a prior employer (or even another company during a consulting engagement), or any other conflicting obligations or limitations? If someone is bringing intellectual property to the venture, does she own it? Will an employee work part-time or full-time? Co-founders sometimes have other employment obligations (or are working to tie up loose ends).

- What form of employment contracts should be used? These include verbal agreement, a simple offer letter, or a detailed employment agreement. Detailed employment agreements can run from a few pages to more than twenty. You might use a fairly detailed agreement for co-founders, and an offer letter for most other employees. It pays to be

clear in any agreement, however, long contracts
are often costly and take time to negotiate.

- Will compensation start getting paid right away,
or will it begin once some event occurs, such as a
financing? Often, a start-up team agrees to accrue
and defer salaries – meaning that they're earning
pay, which is building up, but not actually getting
a paycheck for some period of time. What event
triggers the actual payment of salaries going
forward? How will accrued salary be paid off – in
a lump sum, or over time? If a financing round is
the trigger event, what is the threshold amount?
The business will need a lot more than what you
owe yourself in accrued pay – no investor is going
to hand over money just so a team can pay itself
for work that's already complete (and in any case
be sure to discuss compensation and back pay
with your investors). What happens if a founder
leaves prior to getting paid? All of this should be
discussed and clearly detailed in any agreement.

- While the start-up process has you thinking about
the upside, don't forget about termination. Every
relationship must come to an end sooner or later,
by choice or other circumstance, and it's best to be

prepared. Is the employment "at will", meaning that the employment can be terminated at any time by either party – the employee or company? Or are there clearly defined criteria and a process for ending the relationship. Often, employment agreements address whether termination of one's employment is "for cause" or not. If termination is for cause (a term that should be defined in the agreement), or if one voluntarily leaves a venture, then no severance benefits are usually paid. If an employee is asked to leave without cause, or leaves for good reason (breach of his employment agreement, for example), then severance benefits would be paid. The issue of stock ownership must also be addressed relative to termination. In any case, this is a complex topic that benefits from the assistance of experienced legal counsel.

• If you anticipate a big team, it may be useful to create guidelines and policies regarding salaries, equity, vesting provisions, benefits, etc. This can save a lot of time and decision-making later on – you can tell prospective employees that all team members are being compensated according to the policy. Assuming the terms are fair and sensible, this could save a lot of time and expense.

Keep in mind that an employee's relationship is between that individual and the company. When negotiating any employment agreement, you will need to think about the interests of the company first. For example, if you are working with a team of co-founders, everyone should do their best to minimize the deferred salary burden on the company. In other words, if five co-founders are accruing full salaries for the many months that it takes to organize and fund the company, expecting to get large lump sum payments at the time of funding, investors might balk – why should their investment go toward anything other than building the business going forward – the founders time and effort is reflected in the equity that they retain in the venture (or so one argument goes)? The flip side, of course, is that we all expect to get paid and stock doesn't pay the rent. Take care to structure agreements that are fair and balanced to employees and future investors.

Consultant: I use the term "consultant" to mean someone who is actively involved in a venture and receiving pay, but who cannot or does not want to be an employee. This arises when a consultant may have other obligations, such as a full-time job or other consulting arrangements. From a legal point of view, a consultant has the freedom to work on other projects (but you're advised to consider limiting this freedom to non-competing projects for some period of time). Consultants do not receive benefits, and consulting income is considered self-employment income and subject to a higher tax rate – although there are no payroll deductions. Most often, consulting agreements are entered into with people who benefit the company, but who are not able to either give their full time and effort, or else who have other restrictions that preclude them from employment. One example is the individual who is helpful getting a business launched, but whose services (such as helping to build a prototype) will not be required a few months from now. Another example is the professor who has contributed technology to a start-up venture, but who otherwise has a full-time job with a university. Employment with a university will preclude a full-time job with the new company, but usually not a consulting agreement for a half-day (or more) each week. Such agreements can be structured so that the consultant provides well defined services to the company, or it can be general and open-ended. With regard to compensation (cash and/or equity), you need to be clear about amounts and timing. With respect to amounts, most consultants will expect to earn more than a similar employee on an hourly basis. Also, their compensation can be deferred just like an employee's during the start-up phase, and you'll need to address termination and all of the other issues. Consultants should also receive reimbursement of their reasonable business-related expenses.

Advisor: I use the term "advisor" for consultants that are compensated primarily with stock or stock options (and not cash). These are generally individuals who we rely on every so often for their wisdom, but who are otherwise not actively involved with the venture. Scientific advisors are one possible example (although some of them expect cash). Retired business executives who enjoy serving as mentors are another. Some may be available informally, while others may even be members of your company's board of directors. In these instances, the person does not need the cash, and wants to participate in any "upside" in exchange for their counsel. Depending on how you structure your company, either founder's stock or stock options may be the most appropriate way to compensate these individuals. While advisor arrangements are often informal, it is still recommended that you have written documentation describing the relationship, even if this is a simple confirmation letter from you to the advisor. An advisor agreement or letter should clearly set forth the expectations for the relationship, and the compensation that is being offered. Such documentation will prevent a misunderstanding, which could destroy a friendship or possibly subject your venture to litigation. For example, many companies build credibility by involving well-known people as members of a business or technical advisory board. These people are often pleased to receive shares in the company in exchange for their assistance. Usually, advisors are paid with a token amount of equity – a fraction of a percent to a percent, although I once provided a well known and influential advisor (who was chairman of our advisory board and actively involved in the company) five percent of the initial equity, but this was a rare exception because he was essentially acting as a founder. Finally, before you promise anyone "shares," be aware that stock that is paid in exchange for services will constitute taxable income. You should speak with your lawyer or accountant about the ways to address this issue, such as possibly using stock options. The last thing you want to do is to issue someone shares only to have them discover months later (at tax time) that the piece of paper you sent to them is costing them a significant amount of real money in taxes.

5. Preparing for the Future

Once you and your co-founders are formally established as a team, and everyone is truly committed, then the real work begins. Although you will communicate with your lawyer throughout the start-up process to get the legal perspective on a wide range of business decisions, there are a few more things that you should consider in the early stages. First, review absolutely everything that has been signed to date, and clear up any questions you may have. It is rare for even an experienced entrepreneur not to have questions (including questions about agreements that have already been signed), so now is the best time to ask them and get answers. If any potential issues arise, deal with them now, not after they become problems.

Second, look into liability issues. Check with your lawyer to be sure that you haven't missed anything important. Depending on the actual concerns, if any, you will want to address them. For some businesses, this may mean something as simple as taking extra care with the design of the product or service. Other businesses may require insurance, such as product liability insurance or directors and officers ("D&O") insurance. Learn where it may be appropriate to limit any potential liabilities that exist.

Third, get organized. This may seem like a superficial concern at this point, but I can't say how many times I've seen documents get lost only moments after they've been signed. Whether you have electronic or paper files (both is best), make sure that everything is put in a place where you can readily access the information. You will need to reference various legal and financial documents all along the way, whether confirming the commitments that you have made to an investor or team member, or checking information for your bank. You need to be organized and should file important papers without delay.

Finally, you've been laying a foundation for investment. Assuming that your venture requires outside investment, now is as good a time as any to speak with your attorney about financing strategy, options, and also prospective investors – but first take a look at the next chapter.

Chapter 9
Investment: Tales of Angels and Angst

You've got the madness, your business idea addresses a strong need in the market, you've got a great team, your business plan is complete, you understand the economics of your venture, and now it's time to raise money from investors to really get things moving along.

It's easy to see that you've come a long way, and you feel good about how your new venture is taking shape. It is now time to convince investors to provide you with the funds that will allow you to propel your new company forward – whether you are looking for a few thousand dollars, or several millions. Irrespective of the amount involved, the same concepts apply. This includes the fact that no matter who your investors are, from the smallest angels to the largest venture capitalists, every investor strives to minimize the risk of losing their money, and maximize the probability of a meaningful return. From an investor's perspective, every financing deal centers on these two critical considerations.

How challenging will it be for you to secure investment for your company? The answer depends on a few factors, some of which you control, and others that you don't.

Let's start with the factors that you don't control. These include the general health of the economy, how investors perceive the state of the industry that you're in, the real intentions and desires of the investor you are meeting with, and whether or not he is having a good day. The best defense for any of these challenges is to be prepared. A great team can counter a poor economy, and convince cautious investors to see the light, but a team that lacks preparation will falter on the best of days.

The most critical factors are under your control. These include the quality of your team, the virtues of your product or service, compatibility with the investor that you are meeting with, and your ability to clearly and concisely communicate the reasons why she should make an investment in your venture. If you have arrived at a meeting with an investor, and you can't convince him (or perhaps even yourself) of the quality of your team and business proposal, then it is too late. This is why team selection and product/service validation are emphasized as an early step in the process. If these aren't feeling right, then go back to the drawing board, before you meet with investors. In many ways, your success with investors happens before you ever meet them.

In terms of investor compatibility, the concept is simple. There are different types of ventures and different types of investors. If you're starting a home-based business and need a few thousand dollars to get it off the ground, then do not waste your time trying to schedule meetings with venture capitalists. Similarly, if a risky venture requires millions of dollars in financing, then the local bank is the last place to turn. Compatibility between a venture and an investor is the same as compatibility among people. Invest time to determine whom you should approach in order to make the best use of your time and maximize the chances of a successful financing.

Types of Investors

In general, there are five major categories of investors:

- Founders
- Angel investors

- Venture capitalists
- Strategic investors
- Banks

Founders: This category includes you and all of your co-founders. Although it is tempting to think that all of the financial resources will come from somewhere else, it is even more tempting for an investor looking at such an opportunity to dismiss it because none of the founders are demonstrating their faith in their new venture by accepting any of the financial risk themselves. Making an investment in your own venture is a meaningful sign that you are serious about sticking with it and making it a success, and should be taken seriously. Although the dollar amount of your personal investment is somewhat important, it is perhaps even more useful to create a perception that you are really sharing in the financial risk of the venture, along with full commitment of your ideas, time and energy. Beyond the clear perceptual advantage, there is a personal advantage to making an investment in one's own venture: you will find yourself quite focused and motivated to make the business a success.

As an extension of a founder I will include "friends and family" as sources of potential investment. The reason for this is because, assuming they have the cash to invest, these people will make an investment decision based on their personal relationship with a founder rather than an objective analysis of the opportunity. They're betting on you, and for this reason many entrepreneurs turn to friends and family early in the fundraising process. A suggestion: do not raise money from your friends or family unless 1) there are no viable alternatives at that moment in time, and 2) the dollar amounts will allow you to make progress and move the business forward. In other words, don't just take someone's money because they've offered it, or because Uncle Max believes in you and "wants a piece of the action." After all, if things go well, you are free to share your new wealth with your family and friends. Also, you should be aware that many larger investors (whether angels or venture capitalists) do not like having small investors involved with a business as it can lead to complexities with financing and also a higher risk of litigation. I have seen several deals turned down by professional venture investors for these reasons.

Angel Investors: This is a term commonly applied to individuals with a high net worth who desire to make investments on their own behalf. In practice, there is a legal definition for a "qualified" investor based on his net worth and income (this definition is provided thanks to the Securities and Exchange Commission). An angel can be any person who meets this definition and has cash to burn. Angels come in all shapes and sizes. While some act alone, others run in packs, often teaming up as part of an "angel network" so that they can review more deals and compare notes. There are several advantages to working with one or more angel investors. First, they're relatively easy to approach, and you can usually find your way to them. A call or email typically gets a reply, especially if you either know the angel, or if a mutual friend (or your lawyer, for example) has made the introduction. Second, angels are typically more willing to listen and provide feedback. For example, while a venture capital firm may dismiss you outright during your first phone call, an angel is more likely to meet with you and provide some friendly guidance, irrespective of any investment. Since many ventures don't warrant venture capital financing, angels are perfect for smaller amounts of investment, sometimes even if these small amounts run into the millions of dollars. The disadvantages of angel investors include the fact that they don't have bottomless pockets, as compared with some venture capital firms (who can generally invest more money into a venture as time goes on), and some angels may not possess the "value added" capabilities or expertise that come with the professional venture firms, especially those with solid reputations. On the other hand, identifying and winning the support of respected angels who have experience in your industry (or who are exceptional business people in general) can be the perfect way to finance a new business venture and simultaneously access expert advice.

Venture Capitalists: Venture capitalists ("VCs") are partners and associates at venture capital firms. These firms work by raising capital, usually from institutional investors (banks, pension funds, etc.), and also wealthy individuals. They pool the money, usually as a limited partnership with the individual VCs serving as general partners. The general partners then make investments with the funds, and shepherd "portfolio" companies to success, usually by means of initial public offerings (IPOs) or sales to larger companies. Venture capital firms vary widely, from those with a few million dollars under management, to funds managing over a billion dollars. While some firms may have one or two general partners, others are large global operations. In general, however, venture capital firms only invest in certain types of ventures that meet predetermined criteria. Some of these criteria are common to most firms, while other criteria are specific to a given firm or partner. Also, since each general partner can only manage so many investments, he or she prefers to make fewer large investments rather than many small ones. In practice, the funding amount depends on the firm, the amount of funds it has under management, the expertise of its partners, whether or not the firm works with co-investors (other venture firms), and other criteria. Many venture firms provide a wealth of information about their funds, partners, objectives, and investment criteria on their websites. In general, however, the advantages of working with a venture firm should be expected to include its professionalism, deep pockets, expertise, and contacts with other experts, firms and executives. The downside is the price. Venture firms are notorious for their pressured negotiations, and their money never comes inexpensively or without strings attached. A practical note: only approach a venture firm if you have worked with the firm in the past, know someone at the firm, or can get a credible introduction. Also, be prepared – you get one chance to succeed. If a VC is interested in your venture, they will proceed with further meetings and "due diligence," which will be extensive. Unless a VC firm agrees to continue to actively build a relationship with your new venture (and start discussing a term sheet for an investment), don't waste a lot of your time and energy running around trying to please them. Many venture capitalists do not like to burn bridges and will never say "no", so consider the absence of a "yes, let's take the next step" as a "no" and spend your time and resources elsewhere. Many inexperienced entrepreneurs become mesmerized by the possibility of working with a venture capital firm until several months later when there's no financing and nothing to show for their efforts. Focus on investors who show active interest.

Strategic Investors: In some special circumstances, other companies can be excellent investors. Strategic investors are companies who take a strategic interest in your new venture and agree to invest with hopes of accessing (or perhaps even someday acquiring) your company or its product, service, or technology. There are two primary paths to strategic investment. First, many corporations, as part of their budgets, have funds specifically directed to such investments. In most of these instances, such funds are targeted to research activities and may be used as a kind of "slush fund" by certain business units. Second, several companies have established their own venture capital funds to seek out and invest in young businesses that are of interest to them, often with the intention of acquiring these companies once they "grow up" and prove themselves. Even certain departments of the U.S. government, including the C.I.A. and the postal service, make strategic investments through grants and other means. The advantage of strategic financing is that it is often low-cost relative to traditional venture capital, with fewer strings attached, and it's sometimes "free" money in the case of a grant. If you're lucky, the investor will lend credibility to your new venture (by association) and possibly become a customer. Many strategic investors will also keep a sharp eye on the investment as a future acquisition candidate. One major downside of a strategic investor is that such investments, especially grants, can take a while to secure, often a year or more. At times this can make strategic investment impractical but it might be considered as complementary to initial funding – the "icing on the cake" that could, for example, eliminate the need for a next equity financing round. The other issue that needs to be considered is the identity of the investor. For example, even though Company X lends credibility, does their investment in any way prevent Companies Y and Z – Company X's competitors – from being your customers, or from considering acquiring your venture sometime in the future? In any case, the bottom line is that strategic investors can benefit almost any business and should be considered.

Banks: Bank loans finance very few start-up ventures. That being said, there are two notable exceptions. First, although a venture itself may not receive financing from a bank, its founders often will. Many home equity loans and personal credit cards have provided entrepreneurs with the cash to finance a new venture. Second, if you have sales (or committed orders), then it may be possible to receive a line of credit from a bank. Every banking relationship has a cost, but this cost should be compared to that of equity (selling more shares to investors). Bank loans need to get repaid on time, but equity consumes a slice of your venture's value forevermore. For example, you might get $X by selling Y shares (representing a certain percent ownership in your new venture) or you could possibly get a loan for the same amount in which case 1) you need to repay the loan, but 2) you don't give up any further equity. Consider using bank debt when you have the revenue coming in and are confident that a loan can be repaid in a timely manner (when you have a temporary need for cash while waiting for customers to pay for their purchases, for example), or are otherwise reasonably sure of your venture's impending financial success. Of course, banks can provide other services, such as lines of credit, once your business is up and running. Some bankers may also be helpful with introductions to investors. Don't get frustrated if a bank doesn't finance your business on day one – it's not their business. Stay on good terms with the bankers you meet. You'll need and appreciate their services someday.

Everybody else: Although I did not list "everybody else" in my above list of the five major categories of investors, entrepreneurs benefit from creative thinking, especially relating to financing. Many new ventures and unproven entrepreneurs will find it challenging (and in some cases impossible) to secure financing from angels and venture capital investors. Furthermore, banks are conservative, meaning that if you don't already have the assets to use as collateral, then you are unlikely to get a loan. If all else fails, don't give up. Look elsewhere. Money is out there and you are likely to find it if you are creative and also persistent. Think out of the box. Consider what you have and how you can use your "assets" to fund your venture. List everyone you know in both your personal and professional life. Speak with anyone who will listen – if someone is not interested in investing then ask if they know anyone else you should talk to. Maybe there is a customer who believes in your new venture enough to pre-pay on an order? Or perhaps you can convince a supplier to advance some supplies to get you started. It could be in the supplier's best interest to help you now – in which case you'll return the favor with your loyalty and future business. Maybe a landlord can be convinced to take a percentage of revenue in exchange for part or all of the rent. Many years ago, I started a retail operation in a regional shopping mall. There was a vacant space that was being reserved for a future chain store expansion. The manager didn't know what to do with it for six months (the six months leading right into the holiday season), and we leased it in exchange for no rent except for a small percent of the revenue we generated. We then worked with a supplier who provided us with inventory on a consignment basis. All we had to do was a small build-out of counter space and various signs. Overall, if you need financing and can't find it from the traditional sources, be creative and find the dollars or resources from untraditional sources. Do not be afraid to ask. A word of caution: untraditional financings can work wonders, but take care that it's a fair deal and that you know what you're getting yourself into.

Types of Investment

As noted above, there are two major types of investment: equity and debt. The term "equity" means an ownership stake in a company. For examples, stock ownership is the primary form of equity investment in a corporation. The term "debt" means a loan – funds that are borrowed by a company and that need to be repaid, most often with interest. In general, equity financing is used when it is desirable to share ownership in a company with one or more investors; debt financing is best when 1) you can get it, and 2) you are confident that you can pay it back. Many businesses use both forms of financing.

Before you set off to secure investment for your new venture, or even to identify the types of investors who you want to meet with, it's important to determine a) how much money you actually need, and b) the financing structure of your company. Your cash flow model will tell you how much you need and when you need it. This will help you (perhaps with the help of your accountant) to determine what form of financing is most desirable for your business and its unique circumstances.

Since most externally financed ventures are incorporated or act like a corporation in terms of the basic principles underlying their ownership interests or "shares," we'll use the corporation as a model for our discussion about financing. The three most used approaches to financing a corporation involve the following:

- Common stock
- Preferred stock
- Convertible note

Sometimes these are used in combination.

Common Stock: When a corporation is formed, it issues shares of common stock. Common stock is the form of stock most often issued to company founders, and it has no special rights or privileges. Sometimes, an investor will agree to accept common stock in a new company in exchange for cash (more often, an investor will expect to negotiate for preferred stock – described below). If an investor accepts common stock, the investor owns equity with no special rights or "preferences," and she stands on the same ground as the founders. From an entrepreneur's point of view, the issuance of common shares is relatively simple. From an investor's perspective, it is also simple, but suboptimal. Here's one reason why: suppose that an angel invests $100,000 for half of the common shares in a corporation, with a single founder owning the remaining common shares – meaning that they each own 50% of the company's issued and outstanding equity. Now, suppose that the founder becomes disabled, the business can no longer operate, and it is forced to liquidate its assets. Although an oversimplification, the founder could walk away with $50,000 of the investor's cash a week after the funds are deposited. Most investors want (and usually get) protection from this kind of situation, and others that could arise. That being said, some angel investors will be fine with common stock, whereas it would be incredibly rare for a venture capitalist to accept it.

Example: A new venture has five co-founders and they receive 2,000,000 common shares at the time of founding. A month later, one of the founders agrees to invest some money to fund the venture. This founder makes the investment in exchange for an additional 500,000 shares of common stock. Since this investor is also a founder, she decides to accept common stock. This company now has 2,500,000 common shares issued and outstanding.

Preferred Stock: Many corporations will eventually issue preferred stock. While common stock has no special rights or privileges, any stock that has different rights or privileges is called "preferred stock". Preferred stock is divided into classes or "series," each one representing a common set of rights and privileges. Each preferred stock series is given a name according to when it is issued, such as "Preferred Series A," "Preferred Series B," and so on. There is no standard as to what any preferred class of stock represents; rather, preferred stock is negotiated on a case-by-case basis. Each preferred class of stock has special rights and privileges. These will typically include protection of the investment in the case of liquidation (such as getting repaid before the common stockholders can get any payment), special voting rights (such as veto power on certain transactions, such as the sale of a new company), the ability to sell or transfer shares in certain situations, rights to access company records, seats on the board of directors, and more (usually quite a lot more). Investors and attorneys who deal in securities matters should have a firm grasp of all of these investment terms (which are most often summarized in a Term Sheet prior to final documentation being drafted), and you should be comfortable with the options and variations relating to the terms of investment in your company. It is critical to communicate with your attorney in order to understand what each term means, and you should never hesitate to discuss the future impact of each and every term. While many entrepreneurs don't understand the subtleties of common terms, you don't want to be one of them. This is an opportune time to educate yourself and protect your future. Special rights to the investors come at the expense of the co-founders (and usually all of the prior investors). Depending on your situation, you can negotiate certain terms, or even make them disappear altogether. Be sure to have the advice of competent legal counsel, and never agree to any term that you don't fully understand.

Example: Three months later, the company in our last example negotiates a large investment with a venture capital firm. The deal includes issuance of 1.5 million shares of Series A Preferred stock. Since the company now has 4.0 million shares issued and outstanding, the investor will own a 37.5% stake in the company. These shares include several rights and privileges for the investor, including a seat on the board of directors; special preference in the case of liquidation; veto power on all major transactions; rights to see company information, and more. The company accepts this arrangement, knowing that these are reasonable terms for the venture capital financing.

Convertible Note: This is a favorite mechanism to secure early investment for a young venture, especially when working with angel investors. A convertible note is best described as a loan that converts into stock at some time in the future, usually at the time of a specified event such as a financing. It is a wonderful investment tool for the entrepreneur because convertible notes don't force you to place a valuation on your company at the time of such an investment. The reason this is a benefit is because if you value your company too low (sell shares at a low price), chances are that the next round of investment will also occur at a lower valuation, and you will live with your mistake forevermore. On the other hand, if you value the company too high for a first equity investor (sell shares at an inflated price), subsequent investors are likely to bring you back down to earth. In this case, even if a second round of investment is secured at a fair value, you're in a rough spot with your original investor who bought high – and who is likely to try to renegotiate his investment or be upset with you forevermore. The convertible note is a great way to bring an individual investor (or several of them) on board quickly and inexpensively. Basically, the corporation issues a convertible note, also known as a *convertible promissory note, convertible debt, or convertible debenture (if someone uses this latter term, you know they've* been at this for a long time). This note represents a loan to the company, in exchange for a promise by the company to pay the money back according to specified terms and conditions. Usually, this means that the money will earn interest and that the principle and interest are scheduled to be paid back in a lump sum at some date a few years in the future. Importantly, the convertible note also includes a conversion feature. This feature causes the money loaned to "convert" into shares of stock upon some trigger event, such as a subsequent financing of a minimum specified amount. When this event occurs, the convertible note converts the loan (original investment plus interest accrued to date) into shares of stock at the price per share negotiated between you and the investor in the new financing. Typically, the conversion occurs at some discount, meaning that the convertible note holder gets a nice price break on the conversion of the loan into shares – as a sweetener for taking a risk and getting involved early on. For example, if the convertible note discount is 10% and the new shares are being purchased at $1.00 per share, then the convertible note holder will receive his shares at $0.90 per share. The convertible note investor, upon conversion, generally receives the same form of shares as the venture investor, such as the same class of stock (usually preferred), and all of the special rights and privileges that come with it. Another benefit of using convertible notes is that a company can issue several notes at different points in time. For example, if investor A agrees to invest today, and investor B wants to invest next week, each of them can sign a separate note which could even include different terms. The primary downside of a convertible note is that some investors don't really understand them, or think that they're doing themselves a favor negotiating for stock in exchange for a relatively small investment. In fact, the convertible note is an excellent way to secure a small or large investment from an early investor with minimal cost and complexity. It can even be used to rapidly secure funds from a larger investor while a term sheet is being finalized for a larger amount. You should discuss the pros and cons of using convertible notes with your attorney, but in general the convertible note is simple (most often a two to four page document), flexible and relatively inexpensive. It can be created, presented and signed quickly, meaning that your business can get its hands on the cash without delay. In contrast, a preferred stock investment can cost many thousands of dollars. If an investor will work with you to use a convertible note, this is often the best way to go.

> Example: Three angel investors decide to invest in a new venture and seek to do so in a time- and cost-effective manner. They agree to invest using a convertible note that includes 10% interest, a payoff date on the loan that is three years out, a 15% discount on the price per share at the time of conversion, and automatic conversion at the first financing round of $1.5 million or more. The final documentation is three pages long, and the entire deal is completed within a week.

Although there are other types of securities that may play a role in an investment, such as options and warrants, stay focused on the basics. Your objective should be to not only get your new business funded, but to do so in a time- and cost-effective manner. Many entrepreneurs get caught up in the thrill of plotting any of a large number of possible financing structures and schemes, but for most ventures and investors, the time-tested approaches work best. These provide a level of comfort for investors, a domain of knowledge for your attorney, and a simple approach that is most likely to get the financing closed with the least expense and in the shortest amount of time.

Making the Pitch

Meeting an investor is like going on a date. Investors get courted every day, and have many amusing stories about overzealous entrepreneurs, and bad dates. It's important to put your best foot forward, and to be forthright and honest. Here's a short list of prerequisites for a successful investor meeting:

- Be on time. If you're presenting as a team, meet early and arrive together. Investors will not stand for entrepreneurs who waste their time and then have the arrogance to ask for money. A show of solidarity also makes a good impression.

- If the fundamentals exist, including a great team with an exciting idea and business model, then you should be confident – so act that way. Keep in mind, however, that there's a fine line between confidence and arrogance – do your best to keep from crossing it even if the investor that you are meeting with is swaggering, smug or boastful.

- Be fully prepared. There's no sense showing up for your one big chance, only to blow it because you don't have any idea what you're going to say. Practice with an audience that will provide honest and constructive feedback.

- Communicate clearly and concisely throughout the presentation, including all slides and written documents. If nobody understands what you are saying, or you get sidetracked for a half-hour, you lose. Some investors will test your focus – do your best to politely keep the presentation on track.

- If you don't know the answer to a question, say so. There is some chance that the investor actually knows the answer and is testing you. Many smart investors do this. Get back to him with a reply.

- Expect interruptions. You're the invited guest and it is not really your show. Go with the flow. Be prepared to cut your presentation short without diminishing its effectiveness. Build extra time into your presentation. If your meeting is scheduled for an hour, plan on time for introductions and diversions – which could take up to half the time.

- Expect rejection. It happens to the best of us for any of a variety of reasons. Learn and grow from the experience. Then regroup, get more meetings, and make things happen. Keep a positive attitude and stay focused on the future.

- More often than not, investors will not show their cards during a meeting, or make commitments on the spot. You may be able to request feedback, but don't push. Stay cordial and leave on good terms.

Ultimately, you should have a vision of where you want to end up with an investor. Sometimes, I'll take a team to meet with a "disposable" investor – an investor that I would never seriously consider doing the final deal with – just for a dress rehearsal. It is amazing how humbling the experience of asking for money can be, especially if you've never done it before. There's little guilt in this since venture investors learn from entrepreneurs all the time. Furthermore, in some instances, you may not be looking for the investor's cash, but rather an introduction to one of their portfolio companies that could be a good partner or customer. Usually, you meet with an investor because you're after their cash. In any case, make your desires clear. Tell them how much money you're looking to raise, and confirm that the investor is investing in companies like yours (preferably before you meet, but it's a good discussion point during an introductory meeting). Be sure to customize your presentation accordingly.

Here are a few practical suggestions in terms of goals, form of presentation, and time frame:

- Know what you want. If you go into a meeting knowing exactly what you want to get out of it, you are more likely to succeed. When you meet with an investor, plan in very practical terms. For example, if you want a commitment for a multi-million dollar investment, then how will you get there? It's not going to happen just because of a one hour presentation. Often, your real goal is a second meeting that involves more of the partners in the investment firm. I would suggest that your goals for an investor meeting should always be people-centered, such as "I want to establish a relationship with so-and-so," or "I need to get her to meet the rest of my team." Think in terms of the people and next steps that are required to accomplish your objective. It's a process – success is all about keeping the process moving forward.

- If it is a one-on-one meeting, consider a flipbook that highlights the major points presented in your business plan. Practice to determine timing. If a few people are involved, either flipbooks or slides (presented on a large monitor, or else projected onto a screen) are preferred. It is a good idea to use slides projected onto a screen for a larger audience. In general, ten to twenty-five slides are optimal – enough to convey substance, but not so many that you only have time to get through half of them. Many conference rooms now have media facilities. Inquire ahead of time, and be prepared to start on time without technical difficulties. If you have a prototype or demo, bring it with you.

- Expect for most initial meetings to run 45 minutes to an hour, although never expect any meeting to go according to your schedule. Some investors like to interrupt and ask questions throughout a presentation (if so, remain focused and get things back on track). Others will stay silent. Both styles have their advantages and disadvantages for you as an entrepreneur. In any case, don't forget why you're there, who you need to impress, and your goals. Also, if an investor wants to talk more, that is a great sign, but do not wear out your welcome. The best deals are usually those that arise out of relationships developed over time.

Closing the Deal

Investments happen because at least two people want them to happen. Never forget that you are dealing with other human beings, so treat them how you would want to be treated. For most of us, this means that we would like to see consistent progress, and be kept fully and honestly informed of how a deal is progressing.

Perhaps one of the most critical aspects for a healthy deal is the concept of actual agreement. Many deals turn sour as a result of a non-existent meeting of the minds. This happens when two parties think (or hope) that they have an agreement, but really don't. Make sure that all terms of a deal are discussed. Many first-time entrepreneurs succumb to a fear of rejection and thus simply avoid touchy subjects. If you don't address such issues head-on, you're likely to blow the deal, or face difficulties later on. A seemingly minor loose end now, especially one that you intentionally avoided discussing with an investor, could turn into something much bigger at a time when it really matters. A good lawyer can help you to see what you are missing and to address any issues.

For more formal investments, such as those from a professional venture capital firm (as well as many angel investments), a term sheet is suggested. This document summarizes the major terms of a deal and sets the stage for the ensuing documentation. I'd highly recommend that a term sheet be used. First, a term sheet ensures that the parties are (literally) on the same page. It includes specific concepts and numbers so that there is minimal confusion about what has been agreed. In fact, a term sheet highlights outstanding issues so that they can be resolved sooner rather than later. Also, a term sheet makes the legal documentation simpler and quicker. An attorney can translate a term sheet into final financing documents in the same way that a builder constructs a home from architectural plans. This will lead to better financing documents that arrive sooner – impressing your investors and providing you with the best chance to keep up the momentum and close the deal on time.

Investment: Tales of Angels and Angst

One of the most important roles for an entrepreneur during a financing transaction is to make sure that it gets closed. This is a point that is often taken for granted, with many entrepreneurs believing that every investor is sufficiently motivated to take care of things, or that an attorney has the deal on the top of her list of priorities. This is almost never the case, and there is a significant need for project management. You should know what needs to get done, who is doing what, who knows what, and the activities that are required to move people and documents closer and closer to actual signatures. I've personally been involved in financings that get bogged down as a result of some seemingly minor detail. In one case involving a 500-page closing document, the closing was held up because a law firm was missing a power of attorney from a single minor shareholder – a virtually insignificant player who owned 1% of the shares in the venture. Everyone scrambled to find him, to no avail. Ultimately, we convinced a houseguest to search around on his desk, find the document, and fax it to us. The five-hour delay made a lot of people anxious, and cost several thousand dollars in additional legal fees. I would suggest that you and your attorney regularly review progress and "open" items. If it's a simple deal, it's no problem to do this. If the deal is complex, make sure that someone is managing it and driving it forward, or you could wind up with an expensive train wreck – and no funding. Your goal is to get the right deal closed in a timely manner.

<u>Follow-Up</u>

Just because you have cash in hand doesn't mean that the deal is over. Your investor is now a part of your life, and someone who is demonstrating his or her confidence in you and your team. They expect to be treated well and to see you making progress. Importantly, don't forget about your obligations to your investors, in terms of board representation, information rights, and other promises. The negotiation is now over, and the investors are now sitting on the same side of the table as you. Make the best of it. Seek their counsel when appropriate. Keep them informed of your progress, as well as the challenges you encounter along the way. Invite them to your company functions. You never know where your next big break or round of investment will come from.

Chapter 10
Entrepreneurial Management

A few hours at the public library will introduce you to the litany of books about management, a fascinating and endless journey of brilliance, drivel and deceit. The books range from a lifetime of management wisdom condensed into a lifetime's worth of pages, to management for the "modern" manager published in the 1960's. There's also a broad assortment of authorities on the subject, from the highly respected Peter Drucker, to Shakespeare, to any of a variety of well-known cartoon characters.

Since there's so much information on the topic, I thought that it would be good to condense some of it into a few concepts to get you started. First, however, let's attempt to understand what management is. This itself turns out to be a challenge. One book, an encyclopedia of business management, doesn't even contain an entry for the word "management." Virtually every source that I reviewed failed to provide a definition of the word "management," except for the dictionary. As Peter F. Drucker states in his classic *The Practice of Management*, even many individuals who are involved in the practice of management are unaware of how it is defined. In its very simplest form, Webster's Dictionary says management is *the judicious use of means to accomplish an end*.

The goal of this chapter is to provide a simple approach to management of the entrepreneurial enterprise. It is in no way an academic or scholarly treatment of the subject, but rather intended to provide a simple and practical tool that is easy to remember and actually use. As you will see, learning is a part of this process, so don't stop with this chapter – make it a point to continue to learn about this important (if ambiguous) topic.

Management Made (Overly) Simple

There are three functions for every leader and manager of an entrepreneurial venture:

1. Know
2. Flow
3. Grow

1. Know

What do you want for your new business? What's your vision of how the venture will take shape? What will your products or services "look" like? Clear answers to these questions mean that you've got a Big Picture in mind. This is a great start; however you'll need to take it one step further. Big accomplishments are made up of smaller accomplishments, or "baby steps," and so you'll need to determine all of the little things that are required to accomplish your key objectives. To have a Big Picture in mind, along with a prioritized list of the many smaller things that you and your team need to do in order to actually accomplish your goals, means that you "know".

Although you can't anticipate all of the steps involved, you can create a list of first steps that will take you in the right direction. For example, assuming that you've got a business plan, some of your first steps may be: legal organization of the company, meeting with investors, finding employees, and all of the other things discussed in previous chapters. Next, divide each major item into its components. The prior chapters in this book provide a good idea of the details for many such activities. This will help you to create your own custom list of activities that you can then pursue in a manageable way.

Once you "know" the Big Picture and what needs to be done, you can then determine who should do it. Often, the person will be you. It may also be one of your co-founders, attorney, accountant, or somebody else. Once you determine who will take care of a particular activity, the next step is to communicate the information.

2. Flow

Flow is two-way communication. Now that you "know" what you need to do in order to be successful, you can "flow" this information between members of your team. Effective flow consists of three critical elements:

- Knowing <u>what</u> information to communicate
- Knowing <u>who</u> to actually communicate with
- Knowing <u>how</u> to communicate most effectively

What: You know what it means to "know" – to have a vision for your business including an understanding of what it will take to accomplish your larger goals.

Who: In most established businesses, employees have clear job titles and responsibilities. This is not typically the case for an entrepreneurial venture. Even though job titles may have been doled out, nothing is perfectly clear, and sometimes everybody seems to be doing everything. You and your team members need to determine who will do what – not the big goals, but the baby steps. Who will be responsible for interfacing with the lawyer? Who will spearhead market research for the business plan? Who will take charge of actually writing it? Who is designing the product? Who is in touch with your vendors, etc? It's critical to have someone in charge, and this individual (you) needs to have the wisdom and fortitude to make decisions, such as when an activity or entire goal needs to be assigned to a single person to "get it done", versus when an activity or entire goal needs to be pursued by the team as a whole. In any case, each specific activity requires one or more people to take responsibility for it, and this is the person (or team of people) that becomes the subject of the flow of information. Once you know what information to flow, and who to flow it to, the next step is to most effectively get your point across.

How: All communication should conform to a few basic criteria. First, it should be clear and concise. Next, be sure that there's a two-way flow. This two-way flow can be a simple reply such as "gotcha – I'll have it done in a few hours," or a more extensive interaction whereby the parties discuss goals and actions, clarify loose ends, and agree on the details of how to proceed. Next, make sure there is a consensus. For some activities it is critical that they not only get done, but are also accomplished in a certain way, or by a deadline. If this is the case, be sure that there is a common understanding and an agreement. Finally, keep an open line of communication. Questions and new ideas often arise during the "doing" phase of an activity, and it's critical for you to maintain a constructive two-way flow of information with your team.

3. Grow

Team members are presumably active and achieving the goals you've identified and communicated to them. This, however, is not the end of the process. Management is an ongoing activity that demands personal and professional growth. This means learning from your actions.

Imagine driving a car along a straight road and only being able to move the steering wheel once every minute or so. You'd crash. The reality is that it's necessary to constantly monitor your situation and make adjustments in order to stay on the road, even when you are driving in a straight line. Now consider managing something as complex as a team of people, all with different styles and personalities, all running around accomplishing different things. Without feedback and nearly constant adjustment, you will never get where you want to go. Whether things are good or bad, the process of learning – being open to the reality of any situation and then being able to make the appropriate adjustments – is invaluable.

Effective management means that you know your goals (including what practical steps you and your team need to take to achieve them), you clearly communicate with team members, and you demand feedback and use it to grow. These simple steps will help you to be an effective manager, and the best entrepreneur that you can be.

Next Steps

Entrepreneurship is an adventure. It's not for the faint of heart, nor for anyone intent on achievement minus the hard work. Entrepreneurship is, first and foremost, about learning and growing. Starting and building a company requires a tremendous amount of knowledge about what it means to be in the right business, who your partners should be, and how to bridge the great divide between fantasy and reality. Successful entrepreneurs know their goals, communicate them effectively, and encourage their achievement. Entrepreneurial ventures benefit society, customers, and members of your team. They also reward the investors who have risked their resources on you and your ability to create something of value. Ultimately, entrepreneurship presents an opportunity to test your personal limits, to challenge yourself to be the best that you can be, and to know freedom.